COURAGE & CALLING

Embracing Your God-Given Potential

GORDON T. SMITH

InterVarsity Press
Downers Grove, Illinois

InterVarsity Press
P.O. Box 1400, Downers Grove, IL 60515
World Wide Web: www.ivpress.com
E-mail: mail@ivpress.com

InterVarsity Press® is the book-publishing division of InterVarsity Christian Fellowship/USA®, a student movement active on campus at hundreds of universities, colleges and schools of nursing in the United States of America, and a member movement of the International Fellowship of Evangelical Students. For information about local and regional activities, write Public Relations Dept., InterVarsity Christian Fellowship/USA, 6400 Schroeder Rd., P.O. Box 7895, Madison, WI 53707-7895.

Scripture quotations, unless otherwise noted, are from the New Revised Standard Version of the Bible, copyright 1989 by the Division of Christian Education of the National Council of the Churches of Christ in the U.S.A., and are used by permission.

Cover photograph: Kaz Mori/Image Bank

ISBN 0-8308-2254-2

Printed in the United States of America ∞

Library of Congress Cataloging-in-Publication Data

Smith, Gordon T., 1953-
    Courage & calling : embracing your God-given potential / Gordon T. Smith.
    p. cm.
    Includes bibliographical references.
    ISBN 0-8308-2254-2 (pbk. : alk. paper)
    1. Vocation—Christianity. I. Title: Courage and calling. II. Title.

    BV4740 .S63 1999
    248.4—dc21

                                          99-048677

18	17	16	15	14	13	12	11	10	9	8
13	12	11	10	09	08	07	06	05		

To my two sons, Andrew and Micah

CONTENTS

Introduction

God calls people. Whether it is the calling of Abraham to leave the land of Ur and go he knew not where, or the calling of Moses, confronted with the burning bush; whether it is the calling of Isaiah, who encountered the glory of God, or the calling of the apostle Paul to bring the gospel to the Gentiles, an awareness of calling is both mysterious and powerful. A calling is always a demonstration of the love of God and the initiative of God; but more, it is through vocation that we come to an appreciation that God takes us seriously.

We can understand the call of God in three distinct ways. First, there is the call to be a Christian. The God of creation invites us to respond to his love. This call comes through Jesus, who invites us to be his disciples and to know the Father through him. To be Christian is to respond to the call to know and love God and to love and serve others. This call becomes the fundamental fact of our lives; everything about us is understood in light of it. All aspects of our lives flow from and find meaning in the fact that we, the church, are a called people. Nothing matters more to us than that we are called. This calling is a gift—an invitation offered to us in the mercy of God to become his people and walk in faith and obedience to his Word. It is, essentially, a call to God's salvation.

Second, for each individual there is a *specific* call—a defining purpose or mission, a reason for being. Every individual is called of God to respond uniquely through service in the world. We can only understand this second meaning of calling in light of the first: when we fulfill our specific vocation we are living out the full implications of what it means to follow Jesus. Therefore, while we all have a general call to love God and neighbor, each of us follows our Lord differently. He calls us all to follow him, and once we accept that call each of us is honored with a unique call that is an integral part of what it means to follow him. The second experience of call is derived from the first.

Third, there is the calling that we face each day in response to the multiple demands on our lives—our immediate duties and responsibilities: the call to be present to my sons when they are competing athletically, or to help out in my local church, or to respond to some other specific and important need that comes before me. These are *my* tasks; they are not burdens, but are those things that are placed before me today by God. The call may be nothing more complicated than helping my son repair his car, but that may be what God has for me today. It may be to teach a class or to be present for a committee meeting. I would not speak of these as my *vocation*—which would be closer to the second meaning of call; nevertheless, these may be the duties and responsibilities to which God calls me today. But not all the immediate and legitimate needs that I face are necessarily my responsibility. I may be "overhearing" God's call to another. The danger is always that these daily and immediate needs would crowd out our capacity to respond to our unique vocation.

All three distinct meanings of *call* need to be understood together:

Called of God: The Three Expressions of Vocation
1. The *general call:* the invitation to follow Jesus, to be Christian
2. The *specific call:* a vocation that is unique to each person, an individual's mission in the world
3. The *immediate call:* the tasks or duties to which God calls each person at the present time

---

The central focus of this study is the second of these three aspects of our calling. I will be using the word *calling* or *vocation* not primarily as an occupation or "line of work" but nevertheless to speak of our engagement with the world in response to God. We must consider this second sense of *call* in light of the other two dimensions noted above. Our vocation is a critical way in which we fulfill the call to be a disciple of Jesus.

We must also consider the immediate duties and obligations we have as Christians, as members of families, as spouses and as friends. The daily demands on our lives are not necessarily threats to the fulfillment of our vocation; they are all part of what it means to be called of God.

Because vocation—the second meaning of *call*—is only one part of what it means to be a Christian, we must see our specific and unique vocation within the context of *all* that it means to be called to be a Christian. This will require that we move away from compartmentalization of our lives. We are whole people, complex people, people who fulfill our callings within the whole setting of circumstances, problems and relationships which constitute what it means to be Christian. I, for example, fulfill my vocation as the father of two sons and as grandfather to one grandson. This is an unavoidable and vital dimension of my life, and I cannot consider and think constructively about my work in the world apart from these realities.

What follows is a guide to thinking about calling in this second sense, remembering that when we think about it in this sense we should do so within the context of all three dimensions of what it means to be called by God.

Part One

TAKE A
SOBER LOOK
AT YOURSELF

One

THE CONTEXT
OF OUR LIVES
& WORK
A Theological
Response

*O*ur world is changing. And this change is having a profound
effect on the way we live, the way we work and the way we
think about our lives and our work. The only way that we can
possibly begin to respond well to the change is to face it honestly. While we
often bemoan it—it inevitably involves losses—what we urgently need is
the capacity to see change as opportunity.

The Crisis We Face
The change our world is experiencing has had and is having profound implications for the way we think about our work and how we make sense of who
we are and what we do. In fact, it is appropriate to speak of this change as a
crisis. Different people experience crisis in their lives and work in different
ways and at different times. But when I have seen it—in myself and my
friends, peers, neighbors and colleagues—it has four distinct dimensions.

A crisis of employment. On a basic, observable and tangible level, our
global society is experiencing a crisis of employment. It is not merely that

there is a large number of unemployed people. Rather unemployment—or better, the lack of employment or waged work—is increasingly part of a contemporary economy. We can expect that a high percentage of the adults in our communities will not have waged worked when they need it. The workforce will be increasingly fluid, and many will find themselves at least temporarily between jobs. Some are or will be left without work because their employers are forced to let people go, no longer able to keep so many people on payroll.

For many, the employment and work situation has changed simply because the economy has changed. It is no one's fault, per se; it is just a reality. Some farmers can no longer afford to farm because the crops they have been cultivating are now available elsewhere at cheaper prices. They can no longer compete given their own labor costs or the circumstances of their situation.

In different sectors of the employment world, there are those who have been unable to keep up with the information and technological developments and have been replaced either by computers or by younger, seemingly quicker, more technically savvy workers.

The days are behind us when individuals in any field of work can feel that they have their employment or position for life. When I pastored in the small city of Peterborough, Ontario, in the 1970s, most people in the congregation could assume that if they were farmers or if they worked for Quaker Oats, General Electric or one of the other major industries in the city, they would be with that company—or in the same line of work—for their whole careers. But that is no longer the case; that assumption can no longer be made.

From Peterborough my wife and I went to the Philippines as missionaries, and again we served with people who took it for granted that they would be missionaries for life. Many missionaries once thought that they would serve in a particular country or with a particular organization for life and that their life-long commitment was a mark of their sincerity and dedication. But increasingly mission agencies are responding strategically to ministry opportunities by deploying staff from one country to another, and global ministry will continue to call for highly flexible and adaptive people. It used to be the case that young people could choose a way of life or a career with a reasonable expectation that they would be doing the same thing for the next forty or so years. This is no longer the case. No one, regardless of vocation or line of work, can make that assumption.

We can think about our context in this way: the economy is changing. By economy, I mean what Wendell Berry describes as "our way of making a living," that which "connects the human household with the good things that sustain life."[1] And this economy—the way we make a living—is changing. The changes are permanent; this is not a temporary blip on the screen. And these changes will affect all of us. Everyone, literally everyone, will have job changes and transitions as a matter of course. Whether we fulfill our vocation in the church or in the world will make little if any difference. The organizations we work for and with will reflect the turbulence in our economy. There will be downsizing, outsourcing, companies that depend on a "just-in-time" labor force, and the growth of temporary agencies and organizations that provide us with employment. But it is employment that will be just that—temporary!

We will thrive in the new economy only when we accept this reality—the turbulence and change—and then embrace it as an opportunity rather than a threat.

A crisis of confidence. But the crisis we are facing is more complex than merely a change in the economy—in the way we make a living. As we take a step back we see that we are also facing a crisis of confidence—caused in part by the change in the economy.

Robert Kegan has written a book, the title of which on its own captures something worth repeating: *In over Our Heads.*[2] The distinct impression we get is that in the new economy we are all in over our heads. Regardless of our line of work or responsibility, whether it is business or child rearing, pastoral ministry or public-school teaching, changing circumstances leave us all with a lack of confidence that we can do what we are called to do. In this new economy it is easy to conclude that no one can say that she is the master of her field or that he is a leader in his discipline or a master of his craft. Not anymore.

I am an academic administrator. I love my work and sense that on the whole I have the experience, the expertise and the determination to be effective. But what I and others in this line of work regularly recognize is that we can never keep up with all that we need to know in order to do our jobs well. The complexities of higher education are such that it almost seems like sheer presumption to suggest that *anyone* can do this job well.

The wonderful word *master* was once used to describe the person who was at the top of her craft—whatever the profession. It was a title that one could work toward, a designation that could be assigned with some degree of confidence to the person who was very, very good at what he did—whether it was watchmaking, shipbuilding, teaching or business management. But in the new economy we are all "in over our heads." Just when we think we have mastered our craft—in my case academic administration and classroom instruction—the circumstances and expectations change. The field in which I work is developing so quickly that I always feel one step behind.

In some cases this crisis of confidence means that people experience failure, setbacks and disappointment. They do their work to the best of their ability, but they are not deemed to have done it well enough. The resulting change in their employment situation—perhaps they are demoted—shatters their sense of competence to do that particular job, even their confidence that they can do any job at all.

Others who are perhaps still employed face criticism or inadequate affirmation and support. They are left with little if any confidence for pressing on in the midst of changes in the economy and their work situations. In some circumstances it is the political pressures of their occupations that have taken the wind out of their sails.

Still others are parents who while raising their families moved out of the waged workforce for a time, and now, perhaps as much as fifteen years later, things have changed so much that they lack the confidence to pick up their careers again or to return to the roles and responsibilities they once had.

Others in pastoral ministry have come to a realization in midlife that congregations are changing rapidly, especially in the way they are governed and in the qualities they seek in a pastor. These pastors wonder if they have what it takes to provide effective religious leadership.

Still others chose a line of work or a career when they were young, but now that they have reached midlife and are perhaps in their fifties, they have found that what they had envisioned as an end goal is no longer there. The land they had hoped to farm for life doesn't belong to them anymore. Or perhaps the career they had anticipated is gone; they had trained for a particular line of work and are now discovering that people are no longer needed in that field.

Yet others have come to retirement and have struggled deeply with what it means to let go of their careers; it is so easy for them to feel like they are being dismissed by the organizations for which they worked, perhaps for many years. There are few things as painful as the feeling that we have been pushed out, and that pain can strike at the heart of self-confidence.

Finally, for some the crisis of confidence comes when grandiose ideals are dashed. A woman who was certain that by the time she was in her mid-thirties she would have made her first million in her own business; a man who went into the pastorate convinced that he would quickly have a congregation that is the envy of all other pastors; the team of individuals who longed to do great deeds for God in the inner city only to see those they longed to serve reject the offer of help. Such people often hold the kinds of ideals that *need* to be set aside. Sometimes there is nothing to do but accept the disappointment and honestly see that our illusions about ourselves are just that—illusions. We are trying to be heroes, and the sooner we let such dreams go the better. But however much we need to face up to our illusions, it is still painful and we will still experience a crisis of confidence. Sometimes it hurts so much that we wonder if we will ever do anything well again.

A crisis of focus. There is a third crisis, not unrelated to the first two but nevertheless distinct. In some respects it is unique to urban dwellers—all those who live in the city or *off* the largesse of the city, which includes farmers whose daily life is ordered by the ebb and flow of an urban complex. It is the crisis of hectic, unfocused activity. People have a remarkable capacity to live overworked and confused lives, caught up in hectic activity that in itself seems to have little meaning or purpose, but that is made up of so many things that "have to be done." This is one of the sins of modernity and of life and work in urban, industrialized societies.

In our disturbed passion to accomplish much and to accomplish it as soon as possible, we have lost a sense of true leisure and of what it means to be reflective and contemplative.

A crisis of meaning. Finally, all of these points of crisis ultimately lead us to a loss of meaning—in our work, in our relationships and in our identity. We all become confused about work and the meaning of work, and consequently we are perplexed about the meaning of who we are.

Some people find that their identity was wrapped up in their work, and forced retirement or the loss of employment leaves them feeling hollow, lacking a personal sense of meaning and purpose. Others know, when they are caught up in hectic activity, that something fundamental is missing. A sense of busyness often makes us feel important. We feed a misguided sense of significance when we make the assumption that if a person is busy he or she must be important or, to turn it around, that to be important a person must be busy. If we are honest, we will see that underlying all of this busyness lies an inevitable awareness that we have begun to lose a sense of what our actions mean and, ultimately, what our lives mean.

As a result of this crisis of meaning, people of all religious persuasions are trying to find answers, solutions and ultimately meaning. Well-written books on work, career transitions and career development are best sellers. There is a palpable sense within our communities that we need to resolve this crisis—that we must come to terms with both our identity and our work so that we can find meaning, joy and purpose in that work.

Various helpful resources are available, but it is most critical that we consider and think deeply about a *theological* response to this crisis in our lives and our work. Many people may consider this idea strange or perplexing because they have not given intentional theological thought to anything. But when a crisis looms before us we have to ask the most critical questions. And here is where careful theological reflection can provide us with a way forward.

A Theological Response

There are three theological foundations that will enable us to rethink and embrace what it means to live and work in this new economy and respond with courage to the crisis. We need to recover a theology of *work*, a theology of *vocation* and a theology of *self*.

A theology of work. The revolutionary message of the Bible is that work is good. Central to the biblical description of the formation of the first man and woman is the mandate they were given to till the earth and name the animals (Gen 2:15, 19-20). They were created to work, and their work was meaningful. God made them workers so that they could be cocreators with him—not in the sense that they were creators of the earth, but in the sense that their work was a part of God's continual re-creation and was therefore important, significant and valued by God.

The Bible celebrates the work that we do in the world. Many of us think of Proverbs 31 as the celebration of a woman, especially a wife. And it is. But I wonder if the central celebration is not actually of her *work*—and of work generally as something that we engage in with energy, passion, joy and diligence.

> She seeks wool and flax,
>   and works with willing hands.
> She is like the ships of the merchant,
>   she brings her food from far away.
> She rises while it is still night
>   and provides food for her household
>   and tasks for her servant-girls.
> She considers a field and buys it;
>   with the fruit of her hands she plants a vineyard.
> She girds herself with strength,
>   and makes her arms strong.
> She perceives that her merchandise is profitable.
>   Her lamp does not go out at night.
> She puts her hands to the distaff,
>   and her hands hold the spindle. (Prov 31:13-19)

Work is good. It is a gift from God. With the Fall and with sin, work became *toilsome* (Gen 3:17-19). But we must never confuse work with toil or denigrate the joy and privilege of work just because it involves toil; we must rather strive together for the recovery of meaningful and joyful work.

Unfortunately we have been deeply influenced by the strange notion that work is bad and should be avoided. Many people live their lives longing to be released from work, looking forward to retirement when they will no longer labor. While retirement does mark an important transition—as I will note in the chapters to come—the longing of our lives should *not* be release from work. In fact, Jesus promises his followers that if we are diligent and careful in small things we will be rewarded with *more* work to do (Mt 25:21). The hope of the new kingdom is not that we will be released from work but rather that our work will be in perfect partnership with God in the kingdom that is yet to come. The prophet Isaiah speaks of the new heavens and the new earth as a place where we will build houses and plant vineyards and enjoy the work of our hands (Is 65:21-22).

Our work, then, is a central expression of what it means to be a Christian believer, a critical aspect or component of our spirituality. Indeed, in many respects our work is a central context for living out our Christian identity. Of course, we can and must affirm that not all work is good. Work can be destructive and hurtful, a disservice to Christ and to others. We violate the very meaning of work when, using the skills and energy God has given us, we intentionally exploit or injure others or merely gratify our own misguided desires. Our longing for meaningful work, then, must be framed in the context of that which is good, noble and excellent, that which enables us to bring pleasure to our Maker, that which we can say with genuine passion that we do "as to the Lord" (Col 3:23 KJV).

I need to add a word about working with our hands. Deep within the psyche of people of many cultures and societies is the notion that that which is *manual* is *menial*. People are inclined to think that work that is done with our hands is less important, significant or valuable than work that can be described as being done with the mind, such as managing, writing, speaking or teaching.

But in the Scriptures we are actually encouraged to work with our hands, and consistently those who are masters of a craft are celebrated, such as those who designed and created the Old Testament tabernacle. Bezalel, an artist, designer and craftsman is actually the first person in Scripture who is said to be filled with the Spirit (Ex 35:30-35). The woman of Proverbs 31 is praised as one who worked with her hands. Our Lord himself was a carpenter, and St. Paul was a tentmaker. There is probably truth in the suggestion that only as we learn to work with our hands, mastering a craft as a means of employment or as a form of recreation, are we truly integrated with our bodies. When we live entirely in our heads we miss out on a major dimension of life.

Finally, a biblical theology of work also includes the explicit call for regular sabbath rest, when we set our work aside and take time for leisure, recreation, worship and fellowship. We are not merely workers; rather we are children of God who are called to work. Our work is never the primary expression of our identity, and through regular sabbath rest we re-establish our identity in God and in his love, acceptance and grace toward us (Ex 31:13-17). We violate the meaning of work when all we do is work, when we lose a rhythm and routine of work and play, work and prayer, work and sabbath rest.

A theology of vocation. Closely related to the matter of work is the question of vocation, and of what it means to have a biblical theology of vocation. I will define vocation more precisely in the next chapter, but for now it is important to stress that fundamental to a biblical theology of vocation is the reality and principle that all vocations are potentially sacred. Whether we are called into service in the church or in the world, whether to manual work or to religious work, to work in the arts or to work in education and the sciences, each call has the potential for sacredness.

If a vocation represents a call of God to serve him in the world, then that vocation is sacred because it comes from God. It therefore makes no sense to speak of a secular vocation; such a phrase is a contradiction in terms. A vocation, because it comes from God, is sacred.

From almost the beginning of its history the Christian community has wrestled with this reality. For the early church, which was deeply influenced by Hellenistic thought, any work that was "in the world" or involved active engagement with society was viewed as secular and probably evil. Thus the spiritual ideal was to leave the world, to be separate from it and to live a life of prayer and study as much as possible. A belief became deeply imbedded in the psyche of the church: that if you had a vocation you were called to leave "secular" employment and to accept the responsibility of service in and through the church.

For centuries it was assumed that one who had a "vocation" was called to the life of ministry in the church, as either a priest or a nun. For Protestant Christians the language has tended to be that of "calling." One was called to the gospel ministry as a pastor or missionary. But this notion is not consistent with the biblical witness, and at different points in its history the church has had prophets who have called us back to a more inclusive notion of both work and vocation.

Noteworthy in this regard is the contribution of the Reformers, particularly Martin Luther, though John Calvin's contribution is also very significant. Both of them called for a spirituality in the world that took seriously the home and the marketplace. They affirmed the common and the ordinary. As Calvin put it, "in following your proper calling, no work will be so mean and sordid as not to have splendor and value in the eye of God."[3] He insisted that all people should have a respect for their own calling.

Both Calvin and Luther refused to make the sharp distinction between sacred and secular that was so characteristic of the medieval world and is still evident in the language of present-day Christians. But Calvin went further and affirmed that each person has been assigned a station or calling from the Lord; this vocation is not something incidental or accidental. Consequently, it is our *sacred* duty to accept and even embrace that to which God has called us. The sacred is not distinct from the secular; rather the sacred is what sanctifies the ordinary and thus makes it good and noble. This idea of sanctification was critical to Luther's assertion that every Christian believer, regardless of station, is a priest.

Luther and Calvin did not go far enough. They were constrained by their social and cultural context, as evidenced by Calvin's diatribe against ambition and by both Reformers' belief that people should accept their social station as something that is of God. But when we view their teaching through a wide-angle lens, we see that Luther and Calvin were promoting a revolutionary idea: that the homemaker, the shoemaker and the preacher all serve God, all respond to the call of God, and thus all have a "vocation."

In spite of the power and influence of Luther and Calvin, the older, unbiblical notion that some vocations are more sacred than others is still locked in our psyches. I remember hearing it suggested when I was a young man that if we really loved the Lord we would be missionaries; and if not missionaries, then pastors; and if not missionaries or pastors, then at least business people (in "secular work") who could support those with the "sacred" callings. Within my tradition this was captured in the words of A. B. Simpson, words that are surely typical of what young people have heard in the past and perhaps are still hearing today: "Your only excuse for staying home and not going to the mission field is if by staying home you can do more to further the cause of missions than by going." While such statements flow from noble motives, I hardly dare to think of what they have meant to many people who, because of that perspective, have failed to affirm and celebrate the sacredness of their call.

Though we have made major progress, this narrow understanding of vocation is not dying easily. We need to thunder from our pulpits and celebrate at every turn in the life of the church that God is calling people into education, the arts, public office, business, engineering, medicine, the service professions—quite literally into every area and sector of human life. We need to proclaim this truth and celebrate it often because the older, unbiblical notion is so deeply imbedded in our corporate consciousness. Further, we need to affirm that only those explicitly called to foreign missionary service should become foreign missionaries. Those who become missionaries when this is not their calling fail to fulfill what it is that they are *really* being called to do.

The recovery of a biblical theology of vocation leads us to a renewed appreciation of the full extent of God's kingdom. All vocations are sacred because the kingdom is not merely spiritual. God is establishing his kingdom on the earth as the whole of creation comes under his divine authority. To that end God calls and enables his children to be his kingdom agents within every sphere of life and society. Each vocation reflects but one avenue by which God, through word and deed, is accomplishing the establishment of his kingdom.

Now it is important to stress that we must still sustain a distinction between vocation and career—something I will examine further in a later chapter. A vocation comes from God, and though it can involve work in any sector of society, from the home to the marketplace to the church, it remains fundamentally religious.

The language of many still confuses *vocational* with *technical,* as though one might attend a vocational school and train for a trade or profession rather than attend a liberal arts school or institution. Ironically, some people seem to assume that if you choose the academic route instead of the "vocational" alternative, you will not have been trained to do something useful! In these chapters I will be using the word *vocation* in a very different sense.

Some people suggest that we should no longer use the word *vocation* because it has lost its original meaning and force. But to stop using this wonderful word would be to cave in to a false notion of vocation. We must recover the original meaning. We must restore to our communities and to our language an understand of *vocation* as *calling*—as something that is fundamentally sacred and that enables us, in response to God's call, to embrace what God would have us be and do in the church and in the world.

A theology of self. We come now to the third key element in a theological response to this crisis we face. Scripture clearly proclaims what it means to have human identity: a person is created by God and has worth and significance. The field of psychology has enabled many people to appreciate the full significance and weight of the scriptural insight. Erik Erikson helps his readers appreciate more fully what it means to become an adult—to be mature in one's personal identity. Viktor Frankl effectively argues that deep within the psyche of each person is a longing for meaning that needs to be expressed in hopeful work and purposeful activity. Rollo May recognizes the essential worth of each person and appreciates the power of crisis and stress to undermine personal identity. He contends that the resulting emptiness and anxiety can only be overcome through the power of love, love that enables us to live with freedom and courage. And Abraham Maslow gives us the language of self-actualization, the ideal or goal toward which each person strives—to realize our potential in our work and relationships, and to be able to do so even in environments and contexts that threaten our capacity for inner strength, authenticity and courage.

It is significant that so much of what these writers are saying in their profound insights is also expressed in the ancient text of Holy Scripture. The Bible affirms the essential worth and significance of each person: we are all created in the image of God, we are chosen and elect of God, and thus we have incomparable worth and significance in God's eyes.

Further, the Scriptures unequivocally affirm the significance of the *actions* of each human person. Our work and our actions make a difference to God. God called Adam to name the animals and till the earth, and since then God has continued to take the actions of each person seriously. From beginning to end the Scriptures affirm the all-encompassing glory of God and his work, but at the same time human activity is never portrayed as meaningless, as mere robotic actions that have no inherent value or significance.

Many Christians consider the human person to be nothing and Christ to be everything. They speak of themselves as channels only. They insist that only if they are "nothing" are they a means of grace; the ideal is to be "but an instrument in the hands of God." These Christians' vision is that as believers we should become less and less, that we should decrease so that God can work. The less of us the better, so that the work of God can be magnified. By implication, you and I are an obstacle to the glory of God.

But is this really what is reflected in the accounts found in Holy Scripture? When I watch Abraham and Jacob contending and wrestling with God, when I see the dynamic personal communion between David and God, when I watch the prophets and see their capacity to even confront God, it is clear that we need to rethink this understanding of the human person.

Contrary to the view that denies the significance of the human person and of human actions, the Scriptures speak of the human person as a coworker, a partner with God—even an ambassador for God (2 Cor 5). Human actions matter greatly; our choices and decisions make a difference. Paul urges Timothy to "fan into flame the gift of God" (2 Tim 1:6 NIV). If he does not, then the gift will not flourish! Timothy is urged to be proactive, to take responsibility for his life and his actions. He is urged to see the significance of these actions; patterns of his life *will* make a difference in the church and the world.

Those who argue that the ideal is for the human person to decrease often do so on the basis of the words of John the Baptist as he speaks of his own joy at the coming of Jesus: "He [Jesus] must increase, but I must decrease" (Jn 3:30). We miss the point if we extrapolate from this that the human person has little if any significance. John was speaking *vocationally*. His work is that of a friend of the bridegroom, not that of the bridegroom. Naturally, when the bridegroom appears, it is appropriate for the friend of the bridegroom to step aside—and this is his joy (and surely that of the bride as well).

We see this principle repeated in the affirmation that we are called to lose our lives if we are to gain them; that if we are to be great, then we must be servants of all (Mt 21:25-27; Mk 10:43-44). Implicit in these words is the recognition that we have a life to give, and more to the point, we achieve greatness by giving our life. If by giving our life we achieve greatness, the assumption is that an individual human life before God has the potential of greatness. When the disciples wondered who would be great in the kingdom of God, Jesus' response was not to scold them for desiring greatness but rather to point them to the way of service. Jesus called his disciples into his service precisely because of his confidence that, in his grace and in the fullness of his Spirit, they would make a difference.

Furthermore, Jesus makes the remarkable statement that his disciples are not merely servants; they are friends. He expresses the extraordinary reality that he is making known to them what the Father is doing (Jn 15:15). We are not merely "channels" or "instruments in the hands of God." We are coworkers with God in the work of God in the world, knowledgeable and informed participants in that which matters to the Creator (2 Cor 5).

In the chapters that follow, I am making two assumptions: that all people are responsible for the choices they make, and that these choices are meaningful and significant. They make a difference. Without God, such a thought leads only to despair—as it has for many twentieth-century existentialists. But *with* God and with faith in God, we are rather empowered by this knowledge. We make our choices in response to God, and we make our choices knowing that God is Lord of the universe and that our choices therefore carry significance and meaning.

Our only hope for a genuine and full response to our current life circumstances is a theology of the Christian life that takes our complete humanity seriously; we must have an intentional theology of human actions and human responsibility. I cannot help but wonder if it is a great fear of Pelagianism—the doctrine that human beings are capable of obedience to God through their own strength and will power—that undercuts our capacity to embrace human responsibility. We must affirm the priority of divine action and grace, but we need to do so in a way that calls us to God's grace and enables us to respond fully to it. As Gary Badcock aptly puts it, "A theology of response does not need to be Pelagian; it need only be a theology in which the reality of the *human* is taken seriously."[4]

To take the human seriously is to recognize the power and destructive reality of sin, and thus the existence of what Paul calls the "old self," which is corrupted and deluded (Eph 4:22). But it is also to embrace the new self, which has been "created according to the likeness of God in true righteousness and holiness" (Eph 4:24). We are called to deny the old self and to live in congruence with the new self, which finds its origin in God's creative act. This is the true self, created to respond to God, the self that is given generously in service, and the self that is found in community.

It is estimated that over 80 percent of the books published in any given year are about the self. We are consumed with our "selves." Some people might consider this volume to be yet another such book about the self. But there is a critical difference: in order to resist being absorbed with ourselves we must find, in response to God's grace, moral grounding, a clear sense of authentic identity and, in the end, clarity regarding our own vocation. Only then can we turn from self-absorption and self-centeredness and know the grace of generous service to others. This book is designed to enable us to make that change—to become fully converted, to move from self-absorption and become selves that are centered in God and true to our own identity and call.

No Regrets

I was the pastor of the Union Church of Manila, an international, interdenominational church in the Philippines. My appointment schedule one afternoon included a visit from a man whom I had met but did not know well. He worshiped only occasionally at the church, since his responsibilities as a missionary normally took him to rural areas on weekends.

His story captured my attention. Here was a man who in midlife felt a profound emptiness. To some degree he acknowledged that he had a spiritual problem, and I was inclined to agree. But as we talked I realized that the issue he was facing was something much greater than just failing to maintain a devotional life. His predicament was not merely the consequence of a pattern of sinful behavior or of neglecting spiritual disciplines. Rather he was experiencing a crisis of vocation and identity.

As he looked back over his life, he questioned many of his choices. With all sincerity he had done what he thought was right, he had sought to be the best he could be in his responsibilities. He did all he could to be faithful in his duties as a missionary, husband, father and Christian believer. But something was not right. He was looking for advice, but even more for someone to stand with him as he thought through the issues of his life.

As we spoke I recognized that though there were specific problems that needed resolution, the biggest issue was that this man was alienated from himself. He was not sure of himself—his gifts, his abilities, his call. He did not know himself; he was not sure of his deepest desires and values. One side of him said that he had ability, potential and a unique call from God. But the other side of his mind sent signals that concerned him—he felt as though he had missed his own life. What to do?

When he left my office that afternoon I made some notes that eventually led to the manuscript for this book. I began to ask the question: what are the factors that make it possible for people to achieve their potential in the service of God and of Christ's kingdom?

From Union Church of Manila I moved to Regina, Canada, and became the vice president and dean of a college and seminary. I had put aside my notes for a while during the transition, but it was not long before they came out again as I interacted with the students I was privileged to serve. I saw talent and ability. I recognized tremendous potential in individuals who had come to study, learn and prepare for a lifetime in the service of God. The question arose again: "What are the factors that will ultimately determine whether these students will achieve their potential?" And my notebook grew.

What follows is a study for people who are prepared to think honestly about their lives—who are willing to acknowledge the gifts and abilities they have from God, willing to be honest with themselves, willing to make some tough choices, and willing to do all of this in partnership with others.

As you read you may be tempted to have regrets about the past. I remember sitting in my Manila church study and listening as the struggling missionary spoke of things he wished he had done differently. Now he saw more fully the value of education and wondered why he had cut his studies short when he was in his twenties. Now he saw the importance of being a perpetual learner and of finding times for renewal and rest at consistent intervals. He went on; he had quite a list of regrets. Before he left my office that day, I looked him in the eyes and stated firmly: "I am willing to meet with you over the next few weeks to discuss the issues of your life, but we must do so without any regrets about the past, because the past is the past and there is nothing we can do to change that." No regrets.

All of us can identify things we wish we had done differently, our mistakes and unwise decisions. But we cannot confidently face the future if we are locked in regret. This book is for people young and old, people who are in college, at mid-career or even facing retirement, who want to make an honest appraisal of their lives. It is for people who want to look to the future and be all they can be to the glory of God and for the well-being of Christ's kingdom. Without regret we will look to the present and the future, conscious of the tremendous potential we have because of the grace of God. This book is for people who want to invest their talents, whatever their number, for God.

What follows is an attempt to summarize accumulated wisdom about what it means to respond fully to one's vocation. I have been impressed again and again by how pertinent all of this is to everyone—not only to missionaries and pastors but to men and women in every walk of life. Not only to young adults but to those in midlife and those in their senior years. Not only to women but to men. The principles outlined in the chapters that follow are universal—equally applicable to all people, regardless of religious affiliation. In other words, while my perspective emerges from the vantage point of Christian faith and I identify implications for Christian experience, individuals of all faith persuasions should find this book helpful.

The Longing to Make a Difference

We long to find and do work that is meaningful, that makes a difference and needs to be done. Further, we long to find a balance between work and leisure, between our responsibilities in the world and in the home, between obligations in the church and in our society. We need to be able to manage competing demands and in so doing manage our lives, our time and our priorities.

We also long to make sense of the organizations in which we work—to know when to accept a position and when to resign, to know how to be engaged with our work in an organization without being "married" to the company.

We all want to grow in our capacity to work with others—with people of other cultural backgrounds and with the opposite gender, as well as with people who are older or younger than ourselves.

Finally, we earnestly long to effectively manage the transitions of life as we move through each chapter of our adult careers.

For each of these points of longing, the way forward is through conscious reflection on what it means to have a *vocation*, reflection based on a good theology of work, vocation and self. What follows is intended to encourage that reflection. The biblical foundation for this study is that we are called to be stewards of the gifts, abilities and opportunities that God gives us. Paul urged Timothy to "fan into flame the gift of God" (2 Tim 1:6 NIV). This study endeavors to do just that by considering these questions: How can we, individually and in community, be all we are called to be? How can we fan into flame that gift of God that enables us to respond with creativity and strength to the opportunities before us?

Two

SEEKING CONGRUENCE

The Nature of Vocational Integrity

*The place God calls you to
is the place where your deep gladness
and the world's deep hunger meet.*
FREDERICK BUECHNER

*W*hen it comes to understanding the identity and role of Christians in the church and the world, we are facing a crisis. It is a crisis of the active life—the life of intentional response to Christ to be in the world and make a difference for God. In the face of this crisis—impermanence in the workplace and the changing character of the gospel ministry—we need to be flexible, resilient and creative. We need to be people who have the capacity to learn and adjust. But in the end, what more than anything else enables us not just to survive but actually to thrive, the most critical thing to which we can give our attention, is to come to terms with our *vocation.* Each of us individually must come to peace about what it is that we are called to do. Nothing matters more than this.

I have already said that the word *calling* can be used in three different ways. First, we are called to be Christians. This is the most fundamental and basic sense in which we must consider the notion of vocation: we have been called to love God and our neighbors; we have been called to live by faith, to trust and obey God. We have been called to live in the salvation of our God and to participate in his purposes of hope and reconciliation in our world.

I also wrote about a third sense of the word *calling:* the daily calling to the tasks and responsibilities that require our immediate attention. We must not disparage the importance of these duties that are given to us. We respond to the needs of family members and neighbors; we respond to immediate crises and to the day-to-day, long-term needs of our children as we raise them. We can and must embrace these opportunities and not resent them or suggest that they keep us from our "vocation." On any particular day we can graciously accept that these are the duties, tasks and responsibilities to which God calls us.

I wrote as well of a second definition of *calling*, something much more fundamental, something unique to each person. Every person has a fundamental calling or vocation. And it is this, more than anything else, that each individual must discover. Vocation in this second sense is a critical means by which I fulfill my calling as a Christian. Yes, I am called to love God and neighbor, but how will this be expressed in *my* life? How am I specifically and uniquely being called to fulfill what it means to be Christian in this world?

In the midst of all the daily demands and duties, surely our heart tells us something that is true: that we have a unique calling and responsibility, something that in the long run is greater than the daily tasks that confront us. This does not mean that those tasks are not important; rather we realize that our lives have a purpose.

Although *calling* can be used in any one of the three senses, from now on, except where I indicate otherwise, I will be using the words *calling* and *vocation* to signify the unique calling on each person's life—*calling* in the second sense. In thinking about *vocation* in this sense, it is important that we not confuse *vocation* with *career, job* or *occupation*. Rather it is helpful, if not essential, to maintain a clear distinction. In some situations it makes sense for a calling to be expressed through an occupation. But for many people this fundamental call of God, their vocation, is fulfilled outside of or alongside gainful employment. This can be true for homemakers and for volunteer workers in a wide variety of roles. Many people do not have a formal or clearly defined career, but *everyone* has a vocation. Therefore we need to distinguish between vocation and career, occupation or job. I can lose my job; I might be released from a position. My career can come to an end when I retire. But my vocation comes from God; it remains. It is not something that I choose or that someone else can give me or take away from me. It comes from God; it reflects my fundamental identity.

Even within the same occupation different individuals might have different vocations. And it is important to appreciate that we fulfill some roles only for a time, for a season, to accomplish something temporary. A person may be a homemaker, but probably only until the children have become young adults. Another person may serve in an administrative role for a time, but it is a role for *this* time, not for the whole of the person's life. While these temporary roles are important—they are a way in which we serve God at a particular time—they do not represent our fundamental identity, our reason for being, our vocation.

There are some people whose vocation will actually be fulfilled outside of their occupation; their occupation is but their means of livelihood. And there are others who fulfill their vocation without being gainfully employed. Some people may not even begin to discover their vocation until after they have retired from a career. Thus it is not something we can necessarily demand or expect but rather sheer gift if we are able to fulfill our vocation through an occupation. For many people a job is a means of supporting life and family; it is often a matter of getting whatever work is available. We must be both reasonable and idealistic. We need to discern our vocations, and we must also discern how God would have us fulfill that vocation within the complexities and brokenness of this world. And we can only discover and embrace our vocation if we individually come to terms with *ourselves*. The discernment we need comes from looking at ourselves and nurturing a capacity for self-perception.

This means that if we are going to thrive in this world, in the social, economic and ministry context in which we live, our only hope is to live a life that is congruent with who we are, with whom God has made us to be and how God has gifted us, graced us, and thus called us. If we are going to be all we are meant to be, this is where we must begin. Ultimately, we are only true and faithful to God our Creator when we seek this congruence.

I come to this conclusion in part by observation—by seeing those who thrive in their life and work, regardless of their vocation. But it is also instructive to see that the Scriptures call us to this emphasis on self-perception. Romans 12 is a notable example of a Scripture passage with instructions and commands that can guide our thinking.

In the first part of Romans 12 the apostle Paul calls for *moral* integrity, for lives characterized not by being "conformed to this world, but . . . transformed by the renewing of your minds" (Rom 12:2). He calls his readers to look *Godward*, to have a godly orientation so that their lives are lived in congruence with the character and will of God.

The last half of Romans 12 focuses the reader's attention on others and on the need for a loving posture and behavior toward them. That is, the apostle calls for *relational* integrity.

This is what makes the middle verses of the chapter particularly instructive. In verses 3-8 Paul calls for introspection; he urges his readers to look at themselves "with sober judgment." He urges us to live in faith and to examine ourselves carefully with the grace that has been given us. And then he calls us to live and work in a manner that is congruent with who we are and who we have been called to be. We are called to godliness, to the integrity of lives lived congruent with God's character, and we are called to relational integrity. But we are also called to live with vocational integrity, to have a pattern of living that is congruent with who *we* are. We have integrity when we are true to our own identity, true to ourselves.

> For by the grace given to me I say to everyone among you not to think of yourself more highly than you ought to think, but to think with sober judgment, each according to the measure of faith that God has assigned. For as in one body we have many members, and not all the members have the same function, so we, who are many, are one body in Christ, and individually we are members one of another. (Rom 12:3-4)

Consider these verses carefully. When we ask the question, "What is God calling me to do with my life, and specifically at this time of my life," we are wise to begin by responding intentionally to the two commands that are implicit in the words of the apostle Paul in Romans 12:3-8: know yourself; be true to yourself. These two commands are liberating and we encounter them not just once but again and again over the whole course of our lives. We are not speaking here of a single action or event or choice but of two ongoing commands. Each of them is important to seeking and discovering personal congruence, and they enable us to respond with strength to the crises, transitions and opportunities of our lives.

Know Yourself

The first command is simply "Know yourself." It is implicit in what we read in Romans 12:3: "For by the grace given to me I say to everyone among you not to think of yourself more highly than you ought to think, but to think with sober judgment, each according to the measure of faith that God has assigned."

The apostle Paul calls us to look at ourselves with "sober judgment." God has granted grace to each of us; therefore, we can take an honest, critical and discerning look at ourselves.

Make an appraisal of yourself—an honest assessment. Think of yourself in truth: *Who am I? What makes me unique? How has God called me?* We are not all the same. Rather Paul compares the community of faith to a body with differing gifts, differing contributions and differing abilities (Rom 12:4-5). Vocational identity is found in discerning who we are within this mix. What is the ability, the talent, the enabling that God has given you? Where is God calling you to make a difference for him in the church and in the world? Consider and think of yourself with honesty; make a sober judgment.

To live in truth, we must be true to who we are. But this is not possible unless we *know* who we are: how God has made us, how we are unique, how God has enabled us to serve him in the church and in the world.

Many of us hesitate to hear this call to self-knowledge; something blocks us. We have been taught all our lives to ignore ourselves—to focus on others and to live for others and to give generously. But we cannot serve with grace and we cannot make a difference for God in the lives of others if we violate who we are. In the same chapter Paul calls his readers to love and serve others. But he *begins* by urging his readers to take a sober look at themselves. He calls for self-appraisal *before* he calls for genuine love; self-appraisal makes genuine love for others possible.

If we seek to be anything other than who we are, we live a lie. To know ourselves and to be true to ourselves is to be true to God. For to be true to ourselves is to be true to how God has made us, how God has crafted our personalities, how God has given us ability and talent. God will call us to serve him in the church and the world; however, this calling will always be consistent with who we are, with whom he created us to be. Know yourself, for you cannot live in truth until and unless you do.

It is helpful to think of self-knowledge as something that we gain when we respond to four questions:

□ What are my gifts and abilities?

□ What is the deepest desire of my heart?

□ Where do I personally sense the needs of the world and feel the brokenness in God's creation?

□ What is my unique personality or temperament?

No one of these questions takes priority or precedence over the others. Who we are and who we are called to be in the world is found at the intersection of all four. But it is likely that one of these questions will stand out for you or will be particularly illuminating as you seek to know yourself and to identify your vocation.

Our gifts and abilities. Self-knowledge and the discernment of our vocation must include, first, a recognition and affirmation of our capacities—our gifts and abilities. The assumption, of course, is that everyone has talent or ability. We are not all equally talented; some are more gifted than others. Humility demands that we acknowledge this. But humility also demands that we accept the talent we *do* have. The parable of the talents (Mt 25:14-30) is a powerful reminder not only of the reality of our talents and abilities but of our responsibility to invest these talents as good stewards. And we cannot be stewards unless we acknowledge the gifts and abilities we have! This is not arrogance or pride. It is true humility—the humility of seeing and acknowledging and choosing to live in truth.

I grew up within a religious community in which people were hesitant to celebrate and acknowledge the abilities and strengths that God had given us. Commitment, generosity and faithfulness were valued, but ability, talent and excellence were downplayed. This orientation was captured in a phrase that I and many of my peers often heard: "God is looking not for ability but for availability."

This was an unfortunate message. It is partially correct and partially false. And it has led many people into occupations or careers for which they are not suited. Their generosity and desire to serve have been genuine but misguided. They have often lived in frustrated failure, wondering about God's faithfulness when they found they were not effective in their work.

It is more helpful to say that God is looking for people of ability who will make their ability available to God. We read in Scripture that God looked for such people, and he still does today. King David was not merely an instrument of miracles. He was a gifted shepherd who could fling a rock with deadly accuracy. It was this ability made available to God, not a miracle, that destroyed Goliath. David went on to make his ability available to God in other ways—as a poet, administrator, warrior-strategist and more. The same can be said of each biblical character who responded to the call of God.

Moses denied that he could speak well, and in doing so he failed to acknowledge one way in which God had gifted him. His was a form of denial and rebellion; it was false humility. Self-knowledge includes and, for some, *begins* when we acknowledge the ways in which we have been gifted.

Some of us are multitalented; we do two or three things well. Still, it is likely that even if we have more than one strength there is a single talent that is closer to the root of our being, to our heart, than any other. This is the capacity that must be activated if we are going to be who we were created to be. Parker Palmer calls this our "birth competency." It is something that is discovered and developed, but it is present in us from birth. Our birth competency is something that is inherent in who we are, part of our essential being. Palmer speaks of it as an "inclination or an instinct that can become a full-blown mastery."[1] We experience freedom when we can get to the root of our identity and discover this inherent capacity.

I need to make an additional comment about perceived weaknesses. We often hear that we need to have a good sense of both our strengths and our weaknesses. While I appreciate what lies behind this idea, it perplexes me that we speak of those things that we do not do well as though they are weaknesses. Why are they called *weaknesses*?

There are definitely true weaknesses in every person—character traits that undermine our capacity to fulfill our potential. But when we say that we must understand both our strengths and our weaknesses, we somehow imply that a weakness is something I do not do well. Why is this a weakness? Just because I do not do something well does not mean that it is a weakness for me; rather it is a limitation or perhaps a "nonstrength." We might say that we do not do a particular task or activity very well; it is not something that we would identify as a strength or capacity. Then we can note that what is far more important is what we *do* do well, where we *have* discovered ability and competence. Those things that we do not do well are simply nonstrengths. Nobody does everything well; what is imperative is that we each discover what it is that we are able to do well.

Before we go on to the other factors that enable us to discern our vocation, I need to make a critical point. When it comes to vocation or occupation, it is essential that we see that it is not merely a matter of aligning one's strengths and abilities with a particular job or employment opportunity. The issue of vocation is far more complex than that because we as individuals are far more complex. When it comes to vocation we cannot think in a kind of linear fashion, in terms of a one-to-one correlation between our training and our occupation. We live and work now in multiple-career societies. What we were trained for perhaps many years ago may be incidental to what we believe should be our focus in the next chapter of our life.

It is essential to see that the identification of gifts and abilities is but one element in the discernment process. It is, however, a necessary and critical component in determining our vocational identity.

Our deepest desires. Second, it is imperative that we ask these questions: What is it that I long for? What are the desires of my heart? What brings me joy? Yes, the desires of our hearts matter. We often think of the desires of our hearts as evil or at least suspect. But the psalmist assures us that God longs to give us our desires: "Take delight in the LORD, and he will give you the desires of your heart" (Ps 37:4). It is sheer hypocrisy to deny the longings that arise when our hearts are at peace with God.

Our desires are twisted and self-destructive when they are shaped by greed, insecurity, a longing for comfort and ease, or an inclination to control or manipulate others (Eph 4:22-23). They can be rooted in pride rather than humility. But when we are right with God and genuinely long to respond fully to him in a way that is consistent with his call on our lives, then we must acknowledge the desires that he has placed in our hearts.

What do we long for more than anything else? What do we long for when we aspire to that which is noble and honorable? When we set aside our longings for security, wealth, comfort, fame and even acceptance, what do we long for? Ultimately our longing will be fulfilled only in the kingdom that is yet to come. But if God were to grant you a foretaste of that new kingdom, what would it look like for you?

One way to identify our desires is to appreciate what it is that gives us the greatest joy. It is worth noting that we will only be effective in fulfilling our vocation if we joyfully do what we are called to do (Heb 13:17). Without joy we cannot be effective. It is therefore very important that we come to terms with what it is that gives us joy, even if it means that we will not have comforts or wealth, fame or power.

Some time ago I participated in an exercise that I found particularly valuable as a tool for assessing what gives me joy. Each of us was asked to list the ten things that have brought us the greatest joy—single events, activities that we have opportunity to do regularly, or things that we used to do.

I listed my ten things. Some of these related directly to my work, like a particularly successful project I worked on with a group. Some of the ten items on my list related to the leisure side of my life, such as my enjoyment of the game of squash, something I had played regularly for over a decade. Others were events—such as the trip my family and I took on the trans-Siberian railway.

Then we were urged to go further and to examine what was *behind* each of these joyful experiences. One man mentioned his love of playing golf but then realized that he did not enjoy playing alone. He enjoyed golf because it gave him an extended time with two of his friends—together in the outdoors without interruption.

We identified what had brought us joy, and then we looked deeper to discover the root cause of our joy. I recalled the project that I had worked on and recognized that the real source of joy was that in this project we had enabled many people to fulfill *their* aspirations. It helped me appreciate my own deep desire—to enable others to be all that they are called to be.

Another question we might ask is this: If I were able to do or be only one thing, what would it be? I remember watching my sons when they were preschoolers. They struggled with having visitors to our home, especially if the guests had small children the same age as themselves. The presence of other children meant that they were expected to share their toys. It was sad to watch them hold all their precious toys in their little arms. They were not having fun, but at least no other children could enjoy their toys!

Yet they were required to make a choice. We would ask them, "Which of these toys do you want more than any other? You have first choice, but you must let go of all the toys but one." It was a good exercise for little boys, an essential part of growing up. In time such situations help us answer the adult questions: If I could only be one thing and do one thing with my life, what would I want it to be? and, What do I long for more than anything? What brings me joy? Get to the root of the matter. Do not try to *imagine* what might bring you joy; seek what fundamentally and actually *does* bring you joy. We must not buy into the lie that joy will result if we have more money or more prestige; we need to know our hearts.

These are but some of the ways we can identify and come to clarity about our desires. The important thing is that we grow in our capacity to be true to who we are by acknowledging the deepest desires of our hearts. Our longings are a key indicator of who we are and what we are called to be and do. They will assuredly be reflected in our vocation.

Recognizing the world's needs. A third key to developing self-knowledge is the realization that each of us sees the world's needs differently. Our vocational identity is aligned in some way with how we uniquely see the pain and brokenness of the world. We all see the brokenness of the world through the very particular lenses of our own eyes and heart.

Often we miss our vocation because our sense of the needs of the world is informed and shaped by the expectations of others. Sometimes preachers or speakers outline the needs of the world in a way that is very compelling. They describe the needs in a way that communicates that if we really cared we would respond according to *their* expectations. But the needs of our world are complex. If we are prepared to listen to our own hearts, we will recognize that we long to help and serve and make a difference. But we must act on our *own* vision for a needy world—a vision informed by our personal reading of the Scriptures, a reading that is sustained by the witness of the Spirit to our own heart.

Where do you see the brokenness of the world? What impresses you to the core of your heart and calls you to be something or do something? When you are able to set aside ego gratification and ask honestly what you long to do to make a difference because you see the need—quite apart from any monetary return or honor that may come your way—what comes to mind?

In Romans 12:6-8 the apostle Paul identifies seven different roles people embrace in responding to the world. My understanding of his list is that these roles correspond to seven different ways of seeing the world and its pain or brokenness. It is fruitful therefore to read these verses attentively and with discernment, asking the question: Which of these most fits who I am and how I see the needs of the world? In so doing we intentionally turn from the propensity to ask how others (especially religious leaders) think we should see the world. Rather, we ask ourselves honestly, before God, how *we* perceive the brokenness of the world.

1. Some, the apostle begins, are *prophets* (v. 6). Prophets see the profound need for people to live in the truth they already know. They respond to the world with a passionate belief that people should live in a manner consistent with their own confession, convictions and values. Prophets call us to behavior that is congruent with our words. All of us believe this is important, but prophets see this as the most critical need of all.

2. Some are *servants* (v. 7); it runs in their blood to be attentive to the practical needs around them. They tend to think that there is too much talk and not enough action. They are often good with their hands. They are particularly sensitive to what needs to be done and are often at a task—even finished with it—before the rest of us recognize that something needs to be done. All of us should be attentive to the needs around us, but for those whose call is that of a servant, meeting needs is the most fundamental passion.

3. Still others are called to be *teachers* (v. 7). Some teachers, but not all, work in classrooms. Some, but not all, are scholars. What makes a person the kind of teacher Paul writes about is the conviction that the main problem in the world is that people lack understanding; if they could just understand, they would know and live the truth! Teachers may even be inclined to think that the world can be saved through education. The rest of us may find this naive. But that is the point—we who see the world differently have a different vocation. Teachers believe that transformation can come through learning.

4. Others are inclined to think that the greatest problem in the world is the lack of hope; their fundamental orientation is one of *encouragement* (v. 8). All of us are called to encourage one another. But some people have a deep-felt conviction that encouragement is precisely what is required if our world is going to experience peace, justice and transformation. They see how discouragement is killing us. Some encouragers use words; they are masters of language and can speak in ways that inspire, renew the heart and give courage. Others recognize the significance of place, and know that the spaces in which we live and work can either undercut or enhance our courage and sense of well-being; they know how to design spaces of nurture, light and life.

5. There are yet others who are active *"contributing to the needs of others"* (v. 8). These are usually those among us who recognize that without funding much that is important does not happen. Sometimes they are even inclined to think that finances make *everything* work! Often they are people who know how to make money, but they are also people who know how to give generously. The rest of us might think of them as a bit one-sided in their thinking; but then, contributing in this way may not be our call. And the contributors are right. We do need financial savvy and generosity to sustain the life and ministry of the church, of nonprofit organizations that respond to human need, of educational institutions and of community organizations that nurture our common life together in neighborhoods. Without the generosity of those who have the means to give, our lives would be significantly impoverished. All of us are called to give generously; but some have the unique ability and vision both to make money and to give it away.

6. Then there are those called to *leadership* (v. 8). There is so much talk

of leadership in our day that sometimes we think that everyone is called to leadership. And just as we are all called to respond in ways characteristic of the other orientations, we are indeed all called to give leadership as required and as the opportunity arises. But some people have a unique passion for enabling others through administration and management, so that organizations flourish, and so that everyone else can fulfill their giftedness. People in leadership are servants of a different kind—bringing together the gifts and contributions of others so that *together* we can achieve something greater than the sum of our individual contributions. They help us see the big picture and help us work together to fulfill our mission, our common vision, and they do so in a manner that reflects the fundamental values we hold corporately.

7. Finally, Paul speaks of those who are called to demonstrate *mercy* (v. 8). While all of us are called to show mercy, some people deeply understand that those around them have a central need for someone to stand with them. They mourn with those who mourn and weep with those who weep. While others may wonder how this solves problems or brings resolution to the issues before us, people who are called to show mercy recognize the transforming power of empathetic identification. They know that the demonstration of mercy is itself life and strength to another person.

My point is that your vocation will in some fundamental way be aligned with how you see the brokenness of the world. It is imperative therefore that you respond according to your own perception of the world's brokenness. It is equally imperative that you not judge others if they do not see or feel the brokenness of the world as you do. They have a different set of lenses; they see the world differently; they have a different call.

Our unique personality or temperament. A fourth essential element of self-knowledge is appreciating that we are each unique in terms of temperament or personality. There are several instruments that can be used to enable people to appreciate and accept their individuality. I have found the Myers-Briggs Type Indicator (MBTI) particularly helpful.[2] Like no other instrument or exercise, it has enabled me to accept who I am, to see that each of us is unique. There is no "right" personality. Our individual temperament is as unique to us as our fingerprint. And to live in the truth is to live in a way that is congruent with who we are in terms of our personality.

And so in what follows I summarize the insights of the MBTI. But I do so only as an example, recognizing that there are various ways in which we can think about personality and temperament. The MBTI, building on a Jungian theoretical foundation, asks us to consider four questions as a means of discerning who we are.

1. Some people are *extroverts* and some are *introverts*. We can usually get a sense of which we are by asking, "Do I draw energy from being alone, or from being with others?" The answer is not a matter of what *should* be, but a description of what *actually* is the case for us. Extroverts are energized by being with people and, as often as not, enjoy being the center of attention. Introverts tend to be more retiring and are quite content to be alone, and when they are with others, they avoid being the center of attention. If you are honest with yourself, which is more true to who you are?

2. Some people process information as *sensates*; some are more inclined to depend on *intuition*. The question to consider is this: "Am I more inclined, as a sensate, to trust clear, certain and concrete facts, or am I more inclined, as an intuitive, to trust metaphors and to think in terms of possibilities, to trust my intuition even more than I trust the 'facts.'" Sensates tend to be more in touch with *reality*; intuitives are more inclined to think in terms of *possibilities*.

3. The next question to think about: "How do I make decisions?" Some people are inclined to decide on the basis of *principle*. They value logic, analysis and justice. Others are more inclined to consider the *affective*—the personal and relational implications of a choice. The former are what the MBTI calls "thinkers," whereas the latter are "feelers." It is important as you think about yourself not to ask what is right or correct; rather than considering how one *should* act or respond, simply consider how *you* are inclined to make decisions.

4. The final distinction is between people who are more prone to seek closure and those who lean toward the spontaneous. The question: "Am I more inclined to live with order, structure and routine, or do I prefer going through life with more immediate delight in the moment." The MBTI uses the descriptive *Judgers* to identify people who are most at ease after a decision is made and who derive fulfillment from the completion of a task. *Perceivers* are those who find more joy in the process—before a decision is

made—and find more satisfaction from starting a project.

These four questions can bring remarkable clarity to our lives by helping us to understand our personalities. Of course each of us is unique: there are sixteen possible combinations of these four dimensions of personality (sixteen different types), and even if we have the same "type" as other people, there are many other factors, such as gender, culture, upbringing and experience, that make us different from them.

This is a very simple summary of the Myers-Briggs perspective, but it can give us an appreciation of the complexity of each person and each personality. Knowing ourselves includes knowing how we are constructed psychologically and emotionally, not just how we are designed physically or otherwise. We are unique, and self-knowledge comes in *understanding* what it is that makes us who we are and in *accepting* who we are.

My appreciation of my unique temperament or personality has, as much as any other factor, given me the freedom to accept who I am and to accept my vocation. Because I am not a sensate, for example, not as inclined to be attentive to detail, it would make no sense for me to be an accountant. Keeping books is not something I would do with joy, and it is something I could not do with integrity in the service of others. It is not me.

We must remember, however, that vocation is never discerned solely on the basis of personality or temperament. There are many career resources that suggest that we should choose our career on the basis of our MBTI score. This is simplistic and reductionistic and, for many, frustrating. The discovery of vocation involves the interplay of all four components of self-knowledge. The understanding of our personality and temperament is essential, but it is only one of four essential components.

Self-discovery within community. Together these four factors—our gifts and abilities, our deepest desires, how we see the brokenness of the world, and our temperament or personality—enable us to discern who we are and what we are called to be and do. But it is also important to stress that our self-knowledge and self-awareness happen in community. We come to know ourselves not in isolation from others but as part of the body of Christ. Paul's assumption underlying his words in Romans 12:3-8 is that we will see who we are within the context of the community of which we are a part.

Community is a vital dimension of vocational integrity. Not only do we fulfill our vocation as members of a community; the very *discovery* of our vocation happens in community. It is possible for the community to be a threat to vocation. People in our family, school, church and elsewhere can communicate expectations that undermine our capacity to know who God made us to be and what God is calling us to do, and to respond to that knowledge. That said, it is in our communal associations with others that we find ourselves.

It is in community that we come to an appreciation of our gifts and abilities—by noting and having others note how we contribute to the well-being of the community. It is in community that we see how we are unique and how the desires of our hearts are different from but complimentary to the desires of others.

It is in community that we grow in appreciation of the needs of other people—within the church and in the world. And it is in community that we see how we are different from others—in our actions and reactions, in our mental orientation and in our personality or temperament.

Self-knowledge is found at the intersection of four realities: our strengths and abilities, our desires, our sense of the world's needs and our personality. And for each of these realities, we can best see and understand who we are when we are in community.

It is important to consider all four factors because any one of them alone could lead us astray. Henri Nouwen forcefully brings this to mind in his reflections about his own vocation.

My trips to Latin America had set in motion the thought that I might be called to spend the rest of my life among the poor of Bolivia or Peru. So I resigned from my teaching position at Yale and went to Bolivia to learn Spanish and to Peru to experience the life of a priest among the poor. I sincerely tried to discern whether living among the poor in Latin America was the direction to go. Slowly and painfully, I discovered that my spiritual ambitions were different from God's will for me. I had to face the fact that I wasn't capable of doing the work of a missioner in a Spanish-speaking country, that I needed more emotional support than my fellow missioners could offer, that the hard struggle for justice often left me discouraged and dispirited, and that the great variety of tasks and obligations took away my inner composure. It was hard to hear my friends say that I could do more for the

South in the North than in the South and that my ability to speak and write was more useful among university students than among the poor. It became quite clear to me that idealism, good intentions, and a desire to serve the poor do not make up a vocation.[3]

There is much that is instructive in what Nouwen says here. First, true humility leads us to accept the fact that it does not make sense, it is not wise, to presume upon God's grace. Nouwen's personality and his make-up were not suited to the work in South America. He did not seek to be someone other than who God created him to be, asking for a double portion of God's grace. Rather he acquiesced in humility to his own identity. Second, he had the humility to listen to his friends, who enabled him to see that he needed to function in terms of his strengths and abilities—his speaking and writing—and that, as they put it so well, he "could do more for the South in the North than in the South." Thirdly, it is worth highlighting his comment that idealism and good intentions do not constitute a vocation—even a desire, however noble that desire might be, to serve the poor.

Self-knowledge and vocational discernment come through the interplay of our response to the four questions. But knowing ourselves and discerning our vocations is only half of the equation. Turning back to Romans 12, we find a *second* command, implied in the first.

Be True to Yourself

The first command is to know yourself. The second command is to be true to yourself. Be true to who you are and who God has called you to be. Fulfill the call of God—*your* call to be who *you* are called to be. That call will be consistent with who you are. Self-knowledge is the critical first part of the battle, but it is only part. The real challenge is to live in a way that is *congruent* with who we are, with how God made us—how he has given us ability and talent, has placed desire in our heart and has crafted our personality—and with how we see the brokenness of the world. Only then do we live truthfully.

The New International Version (NIV) of the New Testament captures well the energy of the text of Romans 12:6-8. Having called his readers to consider themselves with sober judgment—to do a self-analysis—Paul moves forward forcefully in his call to live a life of service. But the apostle's call, in verses 6-8, is to serve in a manner *congruent* with our identity.

> We have different gifts, according to the grace given us. If a man's gift is prophesying, let him use it in proportion to his faith. If it is serving, let him serve; if it is teaching, let him teach; if it is encouraging, let him encourage; if it is contributing to the needs of others, let him give generously; if it is leadership, let him govern diligently; if it is showing mercy, let him do it cheerfully.

If you have been called to be a *prophet,* then *be* a prophet, fulfill your call with faith. If you have been called to *serve,* then serve, without apology, without hesitation, without comparing yourself to others, but with a joyful acceptance of who you are.

If you have been called to *teach,* then teach. Not everyone has been called to teach. Not everyone has the ability that you have. Teach, for that is who God made you to be.

If you have been called to *encourage,* if your unique contribution is to bring hope in dark and discouraging situations, if you have been given the ability to bring light and a new perspective, then do it. We live in a discouraging world and every one of us needs people, at home, in the workplace and in the church, who have this ability.

If you have been called to make money so that you can *contribute to the needs of others,* then do it to the glory of God without any apology to the rest of us who can barely balance our checkbooks. You do not have to apologize for making money. Do it; it is a God-given ability! Only remember, as Paul writes in verse 8, to "give generously."

If you have been called to *leadership,* then again, do not apologize for the call of God. Accept it with grace and humility. Accept the opportunities for leadership that the Lord gives you. But if this is not your call, then beware of the burden of leadership. For it will not be a yoke that is easy, and you will do more harm than good. But if God does call you to leadership, then the Word of the Lord is: "govern diligently" (v. 8).

If you have been called to show *mercy,* may the number of those like you increase. For in a difficult and broken world, a world of refugees, of economic recession and unemployment, of battered wives and broken homes, a world where there are homeless people even in a land of plenty, we urgently need women and men who have the unique capacity to show mercy and to be the means by which we know the mercy and comfort of God. If this is your call, fulfill it cheerfully.

Each of these seven callings represents a basic vocational orientation. And each can be reflected in many different careers, occupations, roles, ministries and responsibilities in the workplace, the church and the home. It is in the roles and responsibilities that are given to us that we accept and embrace our vocation.

If in and through your vocation you have been called to serve in government, then accept this responsibility with obedience. Politics is a noble calling. If you have been called into education, then give thanks to God that you are another one who has been called to educate people, whether kindergarten children or university students, whether in public or private institutions. I will not soon forget a public-radio interview with two men who taught kindergarten in a public school. When it was noted that it is rare for men to be involved at that level of education, they responded by speaking of a call not only to be teachers but to be surrogate fathers to so many children whose fathers were absent. It was a memorable interview.

If you have been called into the arts—as an artist, a musician, an actor, a playwright or a poet—respond eagerly. Unfortunately, many people do not know how to respond effectively to and interact with artists. But ultimately you are fulfilling God's call on your life, not ours. There will be people to encourage you. Seek them out, receive their encouragement and keep to the task.

If you have been called into medicine or dentistry, or called to be a carpenter or a plumber, you have a sacred calling from God. If you have been called to be a servant, meeting the practical needs of others as a caretaker, a secretary or a bank clerk, however your vocation is expressed, then do it with joy, knowing that what you do, you do as to the Lord.

If you have been called into the gospel ministry, then embrace eagerly who it is that God has called you to be. But even here, it is wise to give focused attention to how your abilities, desires, personality and vision for the brokenness of the world affect the way that you serve. Some are called to be church planters; some are not. Some are called to be pioneer missionaries; some are not. Some are called to be teachers and translators; some are not. Some are called to be pastors and preachers; some are not. Even within the gospel ministry there are all manner of roles and responsibilities.

The essential and mature act is simple: come to a full realization of who you are and what you have been gifted to do, and embrace it eagerly. Do it. Be true to who you are. Be true to your call, true to how God has made you. Your call is not a superior call or a more sacred call; it is merely *your* call.

There are many things that could derail us, and we will examine some of these in more detail in the chapters that follow. But first we must affirm two things foundational to vocational integrity: self-knowledge *and* the commitment to be who we are called to be, to be consistent with who we are— our strengths, our desires, how we see the needs of the world and our personality. When we are true to ourselves, we are true to God and true to others; we are living out a life that is congruent with who God made us to be.

The question often arises as to whether our vocation can change over the course of our life. Could it be that a person's sense of identity and calling can change in light of changes either in their own heart, perhaps through conversion, or changes in their environment, in the circumstances around them? While I am hesitant to say that it is impossible for a vocation to change, I have been suggesting all along that vocation is rooted in our fundamental identity—in the essence of who we are. Thus our vocation is congruent with how God has made us. Conversion, or a change of heart and heart orientation, becomes the means by which we discover this identity; it does not change it, but rather it enhances that call. You might say that prior to conversion we lived falsely; with conversion we *find* ourselves and our vocations, though it is certainly possible, before conversion, to live one's true vocation but not in light of the grace of God.

Further, while it is true that we will be called to respond in different ways to different circumstances, I would suggest we simply are finding diverse expressions of the same fundamental vocation. Ideally over the course of our lives we will come to increasing clarity about who we are and what we are called to be, responding to the changes and opportunities in our lives. But our fundamental identity does not change. We merely grow in our capacity to live in a manner that is congruent with that identity.

It is also important to stress that if we are married we must find our vocation and fulfill it as a married person. The apostle Paul takes it for granted that a married man lives with a fundamental orientation toward his wife, and that a married woman is "anxious about the affairs of the world; how to please her husband" (1 Cor 7:34). If we are married, we respond to our vocation in the context of our marriedness and thus work and live with a fundamental commitment to the vocation of our spouse, as well as our own. Husbands and wives are clearly called in complementary fashion. While there may be stress and tension along the way as we negotiate with one another about our understanding of vocation, there is no inherent reason why harmony should not be possible. Both are called; both have vocations. Neither is more essential in the kingdom work of God than the other.

Deep within the corporate consciousness of my culture is the idea that women are called to stand by and help their husbands fulfill their vocations. But all of us, particularly husbands, need to come back to the extraordinary words of the apostle Paul when he reminds us that a husband is called to love his wife as Christ loved the church—he is to give himself for her so that she can flourish (Eph 5:21-28). A clear priority that I have before God as a married man is to enable my wife to discover, embrace and fulfill her vocation, a vocation that will certainly be a complement to mine but which will have an internal and inherent integrity and focus of its own.

The Need Does Not Determine the Call

There is something basic that is implied in all of this: the need does not determine the call. It is simply not possible for it to. Most of us live in circumstances that force us to see and recognize more needs than we could ever fill. I am an administrator of an academic institution; I cannot possibly respond to all the needs around me, to everything that I think must be done. It is not possible. This is true of every one of us—regardless of our vocation or life circumstances. People who suggest that need determines the call are doing nothing but creating an artificial and heavy burden for their hearers.

This does not mean that we become oblivious to the needs around us. Not at all. As caring people we will respond with compassion and generosity to evidence of need. But as people of vocational integrity we do not let the myriad needs around us derail us from fulfilling our *unique* vocation or paralyze us into doing nothing. Neither do we let other people's perspectives of the needs of the world derail us from learning how God is calling *us* to serve him in the world.

Consider the account of Jesus himself in Mark 1. There we read that Jesus had a full day of ministry in Capernaum, teaching in the synagogue, healing the sick, enabling the blind to see and casting out evil spirits from those who were possessed. Then early in the morning he went to a solitary place to pray (v. 35).

Simon Peter and the other disciples came looking for him. They urged him to return to Capernaum because the whole town was looking for him. Jesus was in demand; there were expectations from the townspeople and from his disciples that he would meet their needs. But Jesus said that he would be proceeding to other villages to preach, for "therefore came I forth" (Mk 1:38 KJV). Such a sense of purpose! Such an intentionality to do his work for that day. He knew what he was called to do and the needs around him did not determine the day's call for that day. If even the Messiah limits himself in this way, how much more should we?

We might be tempted to see in this scenario a cold-hearted Jesus. But in the verses that follow we read that in compassion Jesus reached out his hand and touched a leprous man. No, Jesus did not ignore the needs around him. He was *filled* with compassion and responded generously as he was able. But he was not derailed from his vocation.

As the time of his crucifixion neared, Jesus said to the Father: "I glorified you on earth by finishing the work that you gave me to do" (Jn 17:4). I long for the same: that I will come to the end of my life and know before God that I have fulfilled my vocation.

We will not have this privilege unless we come to clarity about who we are and what we are called to do, which includes learning how to say no. This will require focus, discipline and courage. But the result is freedom— freedom from ambition, freedom from the pressures and expectations of others, freedom to be who we are before God. It is the freedom to embrace the call of God upon our lives with joy and hope.

Jesus reminds us that his yoke is easy, his burden light. If a yoke is easy, it means that it *fits* us. It is designed around the contours of who we are; it is congruent with the character, strengths, potential and personality that we have before God.

On some simple but fundamental level, then, our only hope for vocational clarity is that we come to terms with our own heart—with what we individually believe is happening in the very core of our being. Each of us has something that we feel is the very reason for which we have been designed, created and redeemed. In the end we embrace this call, this purpose, because this, so help us God, is who we are. In the end there is something about which we say "This I must do." And we will do it, regardless of whether we have parental approval, regardless of whether we get praise or financial return. It is at this point that we understand we must give up our lives for the sake of others, for only then will we find our lives (Mt 16:25). We live out our calling because we must. And we accept this calling as from God—as that which God has placed in our heart. What drives us is our conviction that God has placed it there. This is vocational integrity and personal congruence.

Three

CHAPTERS IN
OUR LIVES

O *lder notions of vocation and vocational development were
based on the assumption that people wrestle with matters of
vocation as young adults; vocational counseling was provided in
high schools to help students to choose a career.* In a true understanding of
vocation we discover that the same vocational questions actually follow us
through the whole course of our lives: Who am I, and who has God called
me to be? What changes is the way that we consider these questions in and
through the various transitions of our adult lives.

Students of adult psychological development generally agree that there
are three distinct phases in an adult's life. Though we move through these
phases in our own time and at our own pace, there are remarkable similari-
ties, regardless of culture, gender, personality or vocation. What follows is
a simple outline of the phases of adult development—not a sophisticated
analysis but a summary that will help us to think in general categories
about the phases of vocational development.

As you read, keep in mind that vocational identity is a critical dimension of our faith development. For most of us, vocational questions are fundamental to our faith and our growth in faith.

From Adolescence into Early Adulthood

The first transition, and probably the most critical, is the move from adolescence into adulthood. This transition occurs at or around twenty years of age. For many people it happens in the late teens. Others do not make the transition until they are well into their twenties or later. Regardless of when it happens, the critical issue is this: it *must* happen. Personal congruency and vocational integrity require that we take adult responsibility for ourselves, asking and then courageously answering the question: What am I called to be and do?

Few things are so critical to adult and vocational development as a full transition from adolescence into adulthood. It inevitably requires a separation from parents. That is at least alluded to in Genesis 2:24: "Therefore a man leaves his father and his mother and clings to his wife." We cannot become an adult without leaving our parents—leaving them in the sense that we take adult responsibility for our life. I am not for a moment suggesting that we only become adult when we marry, but rather that separation from parents is essential to become an adult, whether or not we marry. And this leave-taking is necessarily emotional; many have left or been separated from parents physically but continued an emotional attachment to parents after marriage, sometimes even across oceans.

Vocational integrity and vitality are only possible if there is a break—a break from parents, from home, from adolescence. But the problem is that this break is often delayed or denied. Parents sometimes prevent their children from moving into full maturity. In his superb biography of Wolfgang Amadeus Mozart, Maynard Solomon contends that Mozart's father insisted on keeping his son in a state of dependency. Leopold "infantilized" his son, and Solomon shows that many of Mozart's problems during his short life were due to his failure to move into full adulthood.[1] This pattern is repeated often, whenever parents intentionally or unwittingly prevent their sons or daughters from leaving them—from becoming full adults.

Often, though, parents are not alone in this game. Young people may play along because they fear the independence and responsibility of adulthood. They remain dependent—emotionally, financially and otherwise—because they find security in the parent-child relationship. They are afraid of growing up, afraid of being on their own, afraid of being an *adult*. But moving into full adulthood is not just an ideal. It is essential for personal and vocational maturity. If we never "leave" our parents, we will tend to remain dependent.

But the problem can be subtler. Sometimes we inadvertently treat the organizations we work for as though they have a parental function. We expect the one who supplies our paycheck to "parent" or care for us. We move into a level of emotional dependency that undermines our capacity to make necessary choices—to leave when we need to leave, to find emotional support outside the structures of the organization, to be true to God's call on us. But organizations will let us down. We will continually feel betrayed by organizations if we do not move out of a parent-child relationship of dependence.

Fundamentally, what happens in the break from parents is that God becomes our Father, our parent. We move from dependence on human parental structures to a mature, adult dependence on our Father in heaven. This is what I long for for my sons—that they would no longer call me father but "brother," for we are children together of God our Father. I am still "Dad" in one sense, but I need to affirm with them that they are ultimately accountable to God and not to me.

There is a very close connection between faith and vocation. In the end we must all choose for ourselves what we will believe and by which faith we will live. While we certainly may have faith as children, maturity comes when we embrace an adult faith, a faith that is our own, a faith that can and does give meaning and focus and purpose to our lives. But it can only be this to us if it is something more than our parents' faith; it must be our own.

Parents have a whole range of expectations for their children, expectations that are often communicated in subtle ways. And the desire to please parents runs deep in the human psyche, so deep that many adults are still in an adolescent mode, continuing to function in terms of what their parents would expect and want, sometimes even after their parents have died. They have not become their own persons. They have not, fundamentally, become adults.

There are many reasons why parents hesitate to give their children the freedom to accept before God who they are and who they are called to be. In some cases this is because of the parents' own pride—their own desire for the affirmation that comes when their children have a particular role or profile. In other cases parents are disappointed with themselves and their own failures and thus hope that their children will become or accomplish what they were not able to be and do.

Some parents long for their children to follow along in the same line of work as themselves. Some medical doctors want their children to enter medicine, and people in business sometimes assume that their children will take over the family enterprise. In some families parents pressure children not to follow in their footsteps but to enter the gospel ministry. While we might be prone to admire a family in which all or most of the children become missionaries or pastors, when I hear of these situations, I am immediately suspicious. It is surely possible that all of them are called to the specific ministries they carry. But they *each* need to know, personally, from God and no one else, that this is what they are called to be and do. They must each know, to the depth and core of their being, that they are doing what they do not to gain the pleasure or blessing of their earthly "father" but in response to who they are, who God has crafted them to be and how God has animated them.

If someone comes from a family in which all the children have grown up to become pastors and missionaries, and humbly and courageously announces that he is called to be a carpenter or a medical practitioner, then the Christian community must rally around him, encouraging, supporting and sustaining him whether or not his parents are blessing his decision.

Most often, probably, parents long for their children to become adults but feel unsure how they can enable their sons and daughters to make this transition. The fascinating field of family theory or family systems highlights the principle of *differentiation.* If we are to mature emotionally, vocationally and spiritually—so that we are not shaped unduly by the criticism or praise of others, so that we are able to live by our own convictions and by our own conscience, and so that we are able to relate intimately with others and even to differ with them graciously—we must come to a distinct and definite differentiation. The root or beginning of this is a mature separation from our parents.

People who are well differentiated are not readily susceptible to flattery or emotional manipulation. Mostly this is the case because they are themselves; they are individuals. As such they are capable of generous service, but they know when and how to say no. Further, they are able to hold their convictions firmly without losing the capacity to learn more or to change their mind. This does not mean that they are gullible; on the contrary, they are able to learn with discernment, to critically appreciate what they are hearing or reading.

The bottom line is a critical need for a clean break from parents. We do not become individuals, we do not become adults, unless in a significant and discernable way we *leave* father and mother. Often, the more defined or strong the parent or parents, the stronger an adolescent's resistance to parental expectations or ideals. Many adolescents in turmoil are merely trying to find differentiation—to establish their own identity. More than anything else they need our patience, understanding and acceptance as they go through this process.

Likewise, the rules and regulations of schools are generally designed to establish a particular pattern of behavior, and the system cannot usually tolerate eccentricity. Often young people who are viewed as rebellious are merely those who will not conform to a prescribed pattern of behavior that is contrived and artificial. Schools certainly need rules; every community needs guidelines to govern its common life. But in many school systems the regulations are rooted in a desire to instill conformity rather than to achieve genuine community, and many young people will instinctively and rightly resist. Some will do it quietly in ways that are less disruptive, and some will resist in ways that harm themselves and perhaps others; but their motives are not necessarily wrong.

Everything I have said about separation from parents is offered with a full awareness that in Asian and Hispanic cultures—and I offer this as one who grew up in Latin America and has lived for much of my adult life in Asia—people tend to stay with their parents longer and on the whole are more amenable or susceptible to parental pressure than are North Americans. At least this is assumed to be true. But my observation is that nothing I have said is less applicable in these settings. Rather because the pressure for conformity and compliance to parental expectations may be greater, this cultural reality only reinforces the need for intentionality when it comes to parental separation.

The break from parents occurs in early adulthood. But there is more to the transition from youth to adulthood than independence. The years of transition are a period of learning and self-discovery. Ideally it should be a time to acquire the formal education that is foundational to life. Many people make the common mistake of assuming too early that they know their vocation and pursue an education that later seems irrelevant. The best advice is simple: keep your options open. Our twenties are a time to learn, to grow, to establish friendships, to begin exploring an occupation, but most of all to get to know ourselves.

Keeping our options open does not mean not engaging in an occupation. Rather it means not specializing too early, not making assumptions too early about what we want to be and do, not fretting if in our late twenties we still lack clarity about our vocational identity. That is fine. We should see this as a time for learning and self-discovery, and, for some, a time to get married and start a family. And when we marry, we should see it as a further opportunity for self-discovery and development, not as another form of dependency, little different than what we had with our parents.

From Early to Mid-Adulthood
If we have made a good and healthy break from our parents and from adolescence, then it is likely that we will be able to navigate the next transition of our adult lives. It will not be any easier of a transition, but we will be able to wrestle with midlife questions on their own terms without carrying the baggage of adolescence through the process.[2]

Students of adult psychological development recognize that the transition from early to mid-adulthood is critical. It happens at different times for different people, but for most it begins in the mid-thirties. Regardless of when the transition comes, it must come. It is a point at which we move directly and intentionally into our vocation, understanding what our vocation is and accepting, indeed *embracing*, the call of God.

Carl Jung, at least in terms of modern psychological studies and insights, was one of the first to profile the significance of midlife choices. At around the age of thirty-eight he initiated a major split with Sigmund Freud, a divergence that was necessary if Jung was to come out from under the shadow of his mentor. There is little doubt that if Jung had not made the break he would not have become such a great psychiatrist. Later he laid the basis for intentional reflection on the middle years of our lives. He noted that our early years—childhood, adolescence and young adulthood—are times in which we get established in the world. For most it is a time to select a career and start a family. But in the midst of these years we must, and inevitably will, begin to ask the fundamental question about our identity: Who, in the midst of all of this, am I?

It is probably fair to say that we do not really know ourselves until our mid-thirties, which is why we cannot make the transition to mid-adulthood—full adulthood—until this time. There is much that we can know of ourselves—our strengths, our deepest desires, the contours of our lives. But clarity for vocational purposes can only come after we have lived with ourselves long enough, and this usually takes us into our mid-thirties. Then we are able to consider the important question: What matters to me more than anything else?

Then we have a decision to make, an inevitable decision: Will we respond to our vocation with focus, direction, purpose and courage? By our mid-thirties we should know ourselves well enough to have a good sense of who we are—our strengths, our desires and our temperament. We should have a good read on what it is that we do that is the fullest expression of our identity.

The decisions involved may be difficult. Many of us will have to say no as much as we say yes. If we are gifted in more than one way, then we need to discern and affirm what is most significant to us and what brings the fullest expression of our identity.

I am a capable teacher and preacher and enjoy both roles thoroughly. I enjoy the classroom and the opportunity to lecture, lead discussions and interact with students. I also enjoy preaching, the exposition of Scripture within the context of worship and congregational life.

However, in my mid-thirties I began to see that there was a third strength that was increasingly significant for me. I realized that I enjoyed

administration. I saw that I was intrigued by the challenge of enabling institutions to fulfill their identity or mission. And friends and colleagues were
increasingly looking to me to play that kind of role. Over the course of a
few years I came to the conclusion that administration and leadership are
probably the *primary* contributions I have to make.

But this involved making a choice. We cannot be all things to all people.
We need to choose, and our choices will mean saying no to some alterna-
tives and eagerly embracing others. This may sound easy, but I know from
my own journey through midlife that it can be characterized by much inner
turmoil. There are some words of Ralph Waldo Emerson that have always
remained with me, words to which I often return, words which for me capture the essence of what it means to mature vocationally through midlife.
They come from Emerson's essay "Self-Reliance":

> There is a time in every man's education when he arrives at the conviction
> that envy is ignorance; that imitation is suicide; that he must take himself for
> better or worse as his portion; that though the wide universe is full of good,
> no kernel of nourishing corn can come to him but through his toil bestowed
> on that plot of ground which is given to him to till.[3]

This captures it! The crux of the matter for so many of us is whether
we turn from envy, refusing to compare ourselves with others and reject-
ing the idea that we are diminished by the giftedness of others; whether
we appreciate that while we will not be all that we would have *liked* to be,
we can, with God's grace, be all that we are *called* to be. Inevitably this
means that we must make a choice—to accept for better or worse who it
is that God has called us to be, and to embrace that calling. Only in
becoming and accepting who we are can we in turn be fully present to
God. This is but another indication of the close connection between vocational development and faith development. But now it is fundamentally a
challenge of midlife.

To embrace our vocation in midlife means that we accept two distinct
but inseparable realities. First, we accept with grace our limitations and
move as quickly as we can beyond illusion about who we are. Second, it
means that we accept the responsibility that comes with our gifts and abilities, and acknowledge with grace what we *can* do. Some of us struggle

more with the first—accepting our limits; others with the second—taking responsibility for our giftedness. But either way this is the heart of the matter—to accept our limitations and to take responsibility for our giftedness.

If we do not make these choices, the failure to do so will eventually catch up to us. My interest in the matter of vocation first arose when I was a missionary. I was in my late twenties and I made it a point to observe my older, more experienced colleagues.

There were three kinds of missionaries, and the contrasts among them were amazing. There were those who were very busy. They lived hectic lives, rushing here and there, consumed with business and what seemed to me to be harried activity. They were the seven-days-a-week people and worked long hours.

The second kind were those who were far from engaged—they went through the motions, but they lacked energy, focus, passion or fruitfulness in their work. Some of these were involved in administration. It made an impression on me that those who were in leadership lacked the capacity to formulate vision, to inspire others and to administer in a way that was effective, efficient and helpful.

And the third kind of missionary were those who were engaged in their work with a positive energy and an abiding joy. Most of all they were effective in their work. And the difference was simple: they knew themselves and they were at peace with their strengths and their limitations.

I am convinced that these missionaries either addressed or set aside the critical matters of vocational identity and choice in their thirties and forties. If we fail to make some tough vocational choices, our indecision will catch up with us in our fifties.

One of the critical concerns of these years of our lives will be the simple but profound question of whether we will be our own person, true to our own conscience and identity, or whether we will sell our souls for the "company." Are you a "company man" or "company woman" or are you your own person? Are you willing to live by your own convictions and your own conscience, regardless of the implications, or will you believe only what the "company" believes? Will you be *you*, or will you live by pretense, by an identity, conscience and belief structure that is not your own but merely one which you think will win you the acceptance of those in power?

What is it that made Florence Nightingale, Nelson Mandela, Rosa Parks and Dorothy Day extraordinary people? They were gifted people, certainly. But the critical factor that shaped their lives was their courage to go their own way and to challenge the system if necessary, even when it meant that they were jailed, marginalized or discounted. They had courage; they refused to compromise conscience.

It is worth noting that many times the expectations of the "company" are more imagined than real. Sometimes they are self-imposed rather than imposed by the organization. Many individuals like to live by the rules and expectations of the organization because they like the security of bureaucratic structures. They speak of the regulations and requirements of the organization in ways that should be challenged, because they are giving official status to policies or codes of behavior that no one is in fact insisting on.

In his superb biography of Samuel Johnson, Jackson Bate makes some poignant comments about the middle years of an adult life. He notes that the middle years, when we face the prospect of old age, are the time of the first major shake-up of our sense of self and identity since adolescence. While some of us may avoid asking the hard questions and facing up to our true identity, the encounter with our true selves can only be deferred, he says, not avoided. Eventually we will be forced to face up to who we are and what we fear. Like many people, Samuel Johnson managed to put off the encounter—to postpone the inevitable by sheer bustle of activity and accomplishment. But eventually it caught up to him as it will for everyone, and it "exacted a fearful psychological toll."[4] The ideal, of course, is that we will embrace this time of change, accepting it as a time to make some tough choices—choices that will require honesty, discernment and courage.

This crisis of identity is fundamentally a spiritual crisis. In terms of our faith development we are far enough along in life to know what matters to us most and what our faith represents—a complete adult trust in God as reflected in our resolve to love God and others. If we face ourselves honestly, doubtlessly we will know that no matter how accomplished we are or how talented or capable or connected we might be, we are not really in control. Facing this and accepting it is fundamental to both our spiritual maturity and to our capacity to embrace our vocation.

Three additional themes that are crucial in our mid-adult years will be stressed in the chapters that follow. One is our capacity to be continuous learners, the second is our capacity to bounce back from and learn from failure and setbacks; the third is a healthy routine of rest and sabbath renewal. All of these themes are crucial to our vocational development in our mid-adult years.

In chapter seven I will be stressing the fact that our capacity to be continuous learners is fundamental to vocational fulfillment. It is particularly important as we move into midlife. This is that time when we resolve to accept whatever we have learned thus far for what it is worth, either putting it behind us or, better yet, building on it. It is the time when we embrace new opportunities, experience new challenges and circumstances that we could not have anticipated when we settled on a career path during our early adult years.

Particular reference should be made to the primary home caregiver, usually, but not always, the mother. If the one who gives the most care to the children has seen their care as her primary role or responsibility, then there is a necessary transition when the children grow up and leave home. We cannot say that our vocation is "raising children," unless we are called to be a foster parent or to work in a children's home. We are responsible for raising our children with care, and it is a noble task to stay at home and care for home and family, but eventually the children grow up, and the primary caregiver will go through a crisis of identity if she does not anticipate this transition.

Women who have not known any role other than that of mother sometimes keep trying to mother their own children and others long after they should stop mothering. Instead, when the children grow up and leave home, the primary caregiver should respond to a vocation and move into a role that corresponds with her strengths, vision and calling. This may or may not be a waged position. Everyone does not need to "work outside of the house" to have a sense of worth. But each person has a call—a vocation. It may be a calling that can be fulfilled in the home, by providing hospitality to guests and travelers, for example.

The point is that though the times of this transition will vary for each family situation, a transition must come when the children grow up and take adult responsibility for their lives. A mother can come to clarity about her own identity, calling and potential even before her children move on as adults, perhaps. It may remain dormant or it may have limited progression in the years of raising children. But as the children grow up their caregiver has a new opportunity to be all that she is called to be.

The mid-adult years are also critical to married couples as they come to terms with the way God is calling them *together*. Some hard choices will need to be made as a couple decides who will be the primary wage earner and whose vocation will be fulfilled more flexibly. Many people step aside in their career development to enable their spouses to acquire training and experience they need to both discover and express their vocation.

Remember, *vocation* is not the same as *career* or *role*. We do not have to be gainfully employed in order to have a vocation. A vocation can be fulfilled in a wide variety of ways and, in principle, every person can fulfill a vocation without holding a position or office or having a career. For married couples this sense of vocation is negotiated as they discover each partner's reason for being, the purpose for their existence, in complementary fashion.

What happens at this stage of life probably corresponds to what Erik Erikson calls *generativity*—that transition in life when we move into emotional, vocational and spiritual integration. This is something that we are not likely to experience fully until we are in our fifties. But it can only happen if we move intentionally into being true to who we are, accepting who we are and living with integrity in light of our identity. We should be wise to recognize that by our mid-thirties and into our forties the challenge of being true to ourselves represents unique choices that we cannot afford to ignore. Only as we accept ourselves and become completely ourselves—without pretense, envy or illusion—are we able to give ourselves fully to God and to others in generous service.

From Mid-Adulthood to the Senior Years
Western societies use the word *retirement* to speak of a transition that occurs in our careers or occupations. For most the assumption is that at age

sixty-five we will "retire" from our role or responsibility. The notion of retirement developed in the 1930s when life expectancy was lower and when it was appropriate for individuals to be released from hard physical work. It was also a time when unemployment limited work openings.

Though many seniors can expect to have healthy, active lives for twenty years or longer after the age of sixty-five, the old notion has remained, and for many people retirement has come to be associated with a life of leisure. But just as many people have come to see that there is something deeply flawed in the idea that one makes a transition from responsibility to leisure, from daily work in the office to a daily stroll on the golf course. What has happened, of course, is that we have confused calling or vocation with career and role. As Christians we may retire from our job or career, but we do not lose our vocation. We can and must continue to discern the calling of God and to ask how he is calling us to make a difference within the options and limitations we will inevitably face.

While in one respect the notion of retirement is inherently flawed, there is nevertheless an element of truth in the concept of "retirement" in our mid-sixties. For there is, within adult development, a necessary transition from our mid-adult years to our senior years. For most people, the transition begins at or around sixty years of age. Retirement from our occupation may signal this transition or be a significant part of the move into our senior years, but it is only one aspect, and for many people it is not the most significant.

This transition, like the earlier two, is a necessary one, for we *are* older and we do not have the same physical capacities. Our role in the church and the world *does* change.

The most obvious external feature of this transition is that we let go of formal structures of power and influence—the roles, the titles, the offices and the occupations—that gave expression to our vocation. We "retire" from *these* responsibilities. The reasons may be simple: we may not have the physical strength or emotional patience or even the desire to hold on to the formal structures or roles that once meant so much to us. What we begin to see as seniors is that our vocations are fulfilled in forms that are more subtle, but, in the long run, more influential. Now we really learn how to make a difference.

For many seniors this transition represents a great opportunity. Many of us will now have the time, the leisure and the financial independence to finally embrace, fully and eagerly, our vocation. Some of us will discover our identity and our calling in ways we never have before. One person I heard talking about his work referred to everything before his "retirement" as but a *prelude*—he finally and with enthusiasm was able to pursue his very reason for being. This chapter in the lives of many seniors is the time when we can finally do what we most love doing.

When we are over sixty years of age we might be only beginning to discover our vocation or to fulfill it in a meaningful way, but we are still called and we do not lose or even really change our vocation simply because of our age. Rather the expression or focus of that vocation, the way in which is it fulfilled, will change.

Wisdom and Blessing

When we are seniors our vocation will have two essential characteristics. The Scriptures speak of two primary responsibilities for older adults: giving *wisdom* and giving *blessing*. First, those who are older are the wise women and wise men of their communities. They contribute through words of counsel, admonition and encouragement. Grey hair symbolizes wisdom (Prov 20:29).

Senior adults long to be heard and appreciated. They long to be recognized. All of our lives we hold platforms or titles or positions or roles that require people to listen to us; and we can assume that we will be heard or recognized. But for seniors now these structures are gone. The platforms are removed. And we are only heard if we are wise—if we actually have something to say that is helpful, insightful and illuminating. This is frightening. Will we be heard? But nothing is gained by clinging to the formal structures of power or influence. We need to let go and learn how to bless.

For the role of the senior is also that of granting *blessing*. Indeed, when we read about Isaac, the patriarch of Israel, we get the impression that the only item on his job description was to grant a blessing to the next generation. We tend to discount the significance of this. We are inclined to think that the really powerful and influential people in a society or in the church are those with the positions, the titles, the visible and obvious signs of decision-making power. But real power comes in the capacity to bless.

I watched my sons mature and grow through their teen years. And one of the questions I asked along the way is this: Who is it that my sons listen and respond to? Who, of all the people with whom they have contact, really influences their behavior? There is no doubt that the answer is found in the idea of blessing. It was not those who used the word *should* when speaking with them—those who have expectations. Rather it was those who enjoyed them, who were generous with time and energy, and who listened to them. It was those who *blessed* them.

It was my privilege a few years ago to be associated with the annual family camp of a group of Christian doctors and dentists who meet together each summer for a week of rest and recreation. I was their devotional speaker on a couple of occasions. My sons loved being part of that camp. When we were there, other men spent time with my sons—on the water, teaching them how to water ski or wind surf, but also in quiet times of conversation. They seemed to have no other agenda than to enjoy and bless my sons and the other teenagers and children who were part of the camp. And they had an immeasurable influence on these young people.

Those in their senior years who have the greatest influence upon the generation that follows are those who bless. We are tempted to think that those who follow us are not as committed, not as dedicated, not as good as we were. We so easily bemoan the apparent failure of the next generation to maintain the values "like we did." But those who bemoan the next generation's shortcomings grow more and more bitter, angry, disappointed and cynical. On the other hand, those who bless not only grow old with grace and joy, they have a disproportionate influence on the generation that follows. There is a time to judge, a time to assess and a time to critique. But I wonder if we don't give up the right to judge the older we get, only because I see that the power of the blessing is so great. Many might read the earlier call to wisdom and feel totally incapable of being a source of insight. But anyone can bless, and when we do we will invariably find that we can be a source of wisdom as well.

A window into this reality is found in the role of grandparents. We often say, sometimes jokingly, that grandparents get all the joy of parenting without any of the grief. They can dote on their grandchildren, bless them, enjoy them, delight in them, encourage them and then not bother to be around when there is need for discipline. But while we chuckle about it, there is an element of truth in the saying: *parents* have the role of disciplining. Grandparents have another role. Similarly, the senior members of the community fulfill their vocation in a way different from others; and at the heart of the matter is their responsibility to bless.

The role of grandparenting itself is for many an expression of their vocation. In his fine study *As Our Years Increase* Tim Stafford notes that the average woman is in her mid-forties when her first grandchild is born. Eighty percent of all women have a grandchild by their mid-fifties, and grandparents over sixty-five have grandchildren who are either adolescents or young adults. Stafford notes that grandparents have many years during which they can have a profound and influential role in helping young people to move into adulthood and maturity.[5] Many people can speak of the powerful and formative influence of grandparents in their lives, and thus grandparenting itself can be a very significant part of this chapter of our lives.

Those who have no grandchildren may ask: To whom can I be a grandparent? We lived for many years in the Philippines when our children were younger, and I often gave thanks to God for the senior colleagues who chose to act as surrogate grandparents to our children. As such they had a formative influence on our sons, largely through their capacity to bless and enjoy them.

To bless is simply to affirm—to take particular delight and joy in someone in a manner that is neither judgmental nor prescriptive. Blessing is often evidenced in the joy that one person takes in being in the company of the other. It is evidenced in the gifts that are given—the gift of time, the gift of opportunities and the gift of skills passed on. It is evidenced when an older person takes a young person to the zoo or teaches a young adult how to repair an engine. But the time spent with the other and the skill passed on is secondary, grounded in taking joy in the one who is blessed, in giving freely without prescription. We must learn how to do this; we must resolve to be people who bless others. For we will not be a source of wisdom—

heard and appreciated for our counsel—if we do not bless. Of the two roles of our senior years—wisdom and blessing—the wisdom follows the blessing.

Letting Go of Power and Control

As I mentioned earlier, I am convinced that part of the essence of vocational identity during this period of our lives is our release of power and control: when we are seniors, people listen to us because we are wise and because we bless, *not* because of our office or any formal structure of power. It is therefore essential that we learn how to let go of power, however easy it is to justify the notion that we are needed in formal roles of power. We need to seek the freedom to let go of control over the people, institutions and organizations where until now we might have had positions of both title and power.

Winston Churchill was a great statesman of the twentieth century, but many have observed that he clung to power much longer than he should have or needed to. In so doing ho did not serve his country well, in effect undermining the very causes for which he had given his life. He hung on to power when he should have graciously let it go. Ironically, there is little doubt that he would have had more positive influence on the events of his time if he had left office sooner. Churchill stands as an enduring reminder to all of us of the critical need to let go of formal positions of power and control, and to allow our senior years to be years of blessing and wisdom. We must remember that are not able to have lasting influence *unless* we let go.

Ironically, Mikhail Gorbachev did the opposite of what Winston Churchill did. Richard Nixon reportedly said of him: "He has decided that he would risk his power in order to save his reforms, rather than risk his reforms to save his power." Gorbachev was the individual who opened the floodgates of democratic freedoms in the Soviet block that eventually led to the end of the Cold War. Nixon's words remind me that many individuals *lose* their positive influence *because* they hold on to formal structures of power and positions of influence.

But we can only let go of the traditional symbols of power if we have learned through the course of our lives that our worth, and ultimately our influence, come from the inside—from the quality of our inner life—rather than from the positions that we hold or the symbols of power that we possess. Our ability to make a difference is rooted in the quality of our lives and in our ability to give wisdom and blessing rather than in any particular role or responsibility we might have.

Incidentally, I am not saying that someone who has turned sixty-five should no longer hold office. Not for a moment. Nelson Mandela assumed the presidency of South Africa when he was well past sixty-five, and it was an eminently appropriate thing for him to do. But I am saying that if we continue in roles of formal position or power, we hold these roles differently and we function differently. When Nelson Mandela assumed the presidency, his deputy actually ran the office of the president, while Mandela's role has been in many respects that of father or grandfather to the new South Africa. Pope John XXIII assumed the office of leader of the Roman Catholic Church when he was an elderly man, but he viewed his role as one of blessing the movements of renewal and change that were opening the gates of reform within that Church.

The essence of vocational transition is represented differently in each of these phases. For young adults it is a matter of taking responsibility for our own lives. For those of us in midlife it is captured in the words of Ralph Waldo Emerson—that we must accept ourselves for who we are, "for better or worse." And for seniors, it is a matter of letting go.

In each case, the issue is fundamentally a spiritual one. As young adults, we must choose to take responsibility for our lives before God, to live as those who respond intentionally to his call. The crisis and choices of midlife are equally as much a matter of the spiritual life. We will only come to a clear sense of vocation if we develop a deeper spiritual life, one from which we can not only accept our limitations with grace but also embrace how God has gifted us. And the transition of the senior years, the transition of letting go, will only be possible if our identity is ultimately tied to God and not to our work and our position in the world. It is, again, a test of the quality of our spiritual depth and integrity.

The Dynamic Character of Vocation

Vocation matures and develops. It evolves to a fuller level of expression. It changes focus in response to changes in our life circumstances as we mature emotionally, as we grow older and experience physical changes, and as we see ourselves and our world differently.

In the chapters that follow we will explore the different factors that make for vocational integrity and vitality. It is most helpful to realize that though these factors are important for everyone, each of us wrestles with vocation differently, depending on where we are in our adult development. Further, we will find that at different points in our life the focus of our work may involve different combinations of our strengths and abilities in various situations and at various times. This may happen in ways that come to make sense only in retrospect, in ways that could never have been planned or even anticipated.

Here is where the realities of the new economy are actually profoundly positive. For many people full self-discovery will only come when we are forced to let go of one role or place of work and respond to a new challenge or opportunity. The fact that change is unavoidable confirms again that we cannot be reduced to a particular role and that we will have to adapt ourselves to new situations and challenges.

At each transition we wrestle with fundamental matters of faith. As young adults we choose a faith of our own to give purpose and direction to our lives. In midlife we trust God with the character and meaning of our lives when we are not all that we hoped we would be; we learn to trust God in the midst of our limitations. In our senior years we find that the only way we can let go is through a fundamental faith in God, a God who is bigger than our work, our career and our ministry.

Vocational discernment and development is not just about occupational choice. We make sense of the whole of our lives in the context of each dimension of life and work and relationships. We consider and reflect on occupational choices, possibilities or problems in the context of everything that we are—parents, church members, community residents and volunteers. As we think about work or ministry opportunities, we think about them in light of everything that we are called to be and do as Christian believers. We also think about our call, our vocation, in light of the immediate priorities and circumstances of our life.

Regardless of what I might do in the long haul, for this chapter of my life I may see that I need to embrace the opportunity to be a parent or to respond to a current need because God is clearly putting it before me. Then I must trust God, with patience and humility, for the opportunities and responsibilities ahead that reflect more fundamentally who I am called to be and what I am called to do.

At each phase of life we need to ask, What is the one thing that I must do *now*? What are my vocational priorities for this chapter of my life? And we answer this in light of our current life situation. It makes a profound difference, for example, if I am the father of four children, or if I recognize that I need to go to school and make a college education a priority, or if I need to go back to school as a midlife transition. *That* then becomes my vocational priority for this chapter of my life. A person's vocational priority might be a fifth grade boys' Sunday school class, if that particular responsibility reflects a central part of who that person is and what he or she is called to be and do. In other words, the most important things we do may not bring a wage, whether it be service in our local church or in our community or in the active support for some environmental cause.

When we do not need to work or cannot find work, we have even more time available for volunteering. For seniors, but also for many in midlife, the challenge is to volunteer in a way that is meaningful. There is an increasing appreciation of the critical role volunteers play in a society and of the contributions that they make. Many essential social agencies depend on competent, committed volunteers to fulfill their mission. All of us should volunteer to do work that is meaningful and makes a difference, but we need to see this work as something that we are called to do, not merely as activity for activity's sake.

Many of us will experience a sense of call at three different times in our life. First, there is typically a sense of call that comes before or during the transition into adulthood—a call that reflects faith commitments. For some people it will be conceived fairly broadly—as a call into business, or medicine, or photography or the pastorate. For others it will be very precise—a definite sense of call to a particular avenue of work or perhaps to a specific gospel ministry. The call is there for everyone, although not everyone recognizes it.

Then, as likely as not, another call will come during midlife, a call that will represent a narrowing of perspective—a focus within the context of the bigger picture. For some people midlife brings a completely new direction. By this time most of us have come to know ourselves, our abilities and our desires well enough to know that we cannot do everything; now we have to choose in response to who we see God calling us to be. This in no way minimizes the first call, especially for those of us who had a very definite and specific sense of call in the first instance. Rather the second call enables the first to be fulfilled and possibly gives it more focus. Naturally, it also reflects a more mature self-awareness.

Third, there is the call that comes as we make the transition into our senior years—a call that is no less significant or momentous in our life than the first two. This moment in our life is significant in part because we are able to hear the voice of God without concern for the expectations of peers or organizations, without the pressures of career or employment. We can genuinely step back and see how our life thus far has been but a prelude to what will follow.

Though there will be different chapters and different calls, there will be a theme or undercurrent that brings unity to who we are and who we are called to be. We may not see what unifies our life until we are older and we begin to look back over where we have been and what we have done. But the underlying theme of our life is there nonetheless, and each chapter will be but one expression of it. Vocational development should not be construed as the single rising curve of misconceived careerism. We are not climbing ladders; we are not doing things in order to make our *curriculum vitae* more impressive. Rather we are working out the story of our life. Our story will include setbacks and failures as well as surprises and responses to opportunities we could never have foreseen.

We embrace the opportunities that come today, often with little idea of the implications down the road. We are not building a career; we are responding, at this time, and in this place, to a call—to a sense of vocation that is congruent with who we are and that ultimately comes from God. And so a homemaker like Cory Aquino may become the president of the Philippines, and the president of a university may step aside and become a writer. When we think in terms of vocation and reject careerism, we can accept with grace that God will call us in ways that would confound people who think only in terms of getting ahead.

Frequently the whole question of vocation is presented in a way that is an inordinate and inappropriate burden. We often confront young people with the question of what they are going to do with their life, expecting that they should know early on and that they should get on with it. But this is oppressive and unnecessarily burdensome.

Young adults are responsible only for the immediate future—not for the whole of their life, or the whole of their future. Further, when we are young, we are wise if we keep our options open, not making premature assumptions about our future, about what we are likely to do as the focus of our life. We can embrace the present with a full awareness that in the future we will probably be surprised by what comes our way.

We must live and work within the context of both the limitations and the opportunities that are current and real in our lives. I am convinced that in principle we should be able to fulfill our vocation anywhere, even if we are confined to a concentration camp. The question remains the same: What needs to be done here? What are the strengths and passions that I can bring to *this* situation and *this* opportunity, in light of the needs and in view of the opportunities before me?

We might sometimes bemoan the fact that we do not have the opportunities that we think we deserve or that we view as essential to fulfill our vocation. But humility and thankfulness require that we simply ask: What needs to be done? Perhaps my spouse needs my attention. Perhaps my child is sick at home this week—or even disabled for life—and I may conclude that my call is to care for that child, for a day or perhaps much longer. Perhaps I am confined to a hospital bed for a long period of time. But I can still ask: Within this limitation, what are my opportunities? Or more specifically: What is God calling me to do here, in this place and at this time, so that I can be a conduit of life and grace to others?

We must be open to surprises as well as opportunities. We fulfill our vocation in community, and we will have different contributions to make in different communities and perhaps in different ways at different times. In one setting I may draw on my gifts as an administrator, but elsewhere it may be clear that others are doing the administration and doing it ably. My calling in that instance is both to encourage them and to perform another role. This is why it is critical that we *not* allow ourselves or others to be reductionistic in the perception of our calling. We should not be reduced to or defined by a particular role or responsibility.

Perhaps you are an Old Testament professor now. It is very possible that this is what you will do for the whole of your active career. But who knows? God is calling you to teach Old Testament now, but there is no need to make undue assumptions about the future. I grieve about missionaries who are convinced that their call to missionary work is for life and find that they are seemingly incapable of rethinking their identity and their call. They have been "reduced" to a particular role or career. The same can be said of any people who define their identity solely in terms of a particular role. At his retirement one wise academic dean gave a talk for other, younger deans and concluded his counsel by saying: "Never let them define you solely in terms of your role as a dean. You are always more than a dean." And this is so crucial for me, of course, when it comes time to let go of my role as a dean.

This is why I hesitate when confronted with tests or questionnaires that are intended to enable individuals to determine their gifts in isolation from a particular situation or set of circumstances. We should always respond to these questionnaires by saying, "Well, it depends." A good case could be made that the "gifts of the Spirit" are given to the church, to the community of faith, and not to individuals per se. Then we can work with the assumption that each community has the gifts it needs to flourish. We therefore must first ask, What gift or strength am I being called of God to use in this place at this time?

Second, we need to ask what we are required to do to keep "alive," especially through learning, but also through friendships, leisure and recreation that prepare us for what the next chapter in our lives might be and enable us to grow in both wisdom and joy.

Third, we must remember this: each transition will involve some kind of loss. Growth will always be costly; a new venture will always involve some form of letting go. It may be a matter of separation—from parents or from those who are part of an old way or an old world. It may involve leaving behind the comfortable and the secure. Each transition will be a small death, and the new life, the new opportunity and the new challenge will only come as we let go.

Once again I must stress: vocation and career are not the same. They *may* coincide, but for many people that will not be the case. At each phase of our life we need to ask the question: Who am I, and what, fundamentally, am I called to be and do? What is my purpose, my reason for being? And then we must ask what we are being called to do *now*, in the immediate: What is the current duty, responsibility or job that God is placing before me? How can I fulfill this current responsibility in light of who I am? The current responsibility or job may seem quite mundane—caring for children, getting a job to pay the rent or studying. But it is God's call for the moment, for the time being. And we accept this as from the hand of God and see it in light of the complete picture of who we are and who we are called to be.

The Heart of the Matter

The heart of the matter, in the end, is found in the answer to a simple question: How is God calling me to serve him at this time and in this place? In chapter two I identified four questions that might enable us to think critically about ourselves—to know ourselves better and to have a better-nuanced appreciation of how God is calling us. But in the end, our knowledge of our vocation is something that arises from our hearts. A vocation cannot, in the end, by discerned by answering questionnaires or filling out forms. Somewhere, mysteriously, in the depths of our heart, God is calling each one of us to make a difference. These questions are meant only as pointers along the way.

The four questions mentioned can, however, help us interpret our own story, for in some sense what we are called to do next flows out of our personal experience thus far. As we consider the next chapter of our life, we do so in light of our story up until now. We answer the four questions in the light of that story and we use the questions to make sense of the narrative of our life—to know more fully who we are and who it is that God is calling us to be.

Furthermore, we always discern vocation in light of the *actual* life circumstances that are before us. This is not to underestimate the possibilities of God's grace; it is merely to affirm that God works in a real world and enables us to make a difference in the midst of our actual life situation.

Finally, the motivation for fulfilling our vocation always remains the same: to bring glory to the Creator and to serve in the world out of love for Christ and for others. Ultimately, a vocation or call is a call to service; if we would be great, we are called to be servants.

Four

AS UNTO THE LORD

The Pursuit of Excellence, Truth, Diligence & Generosity

W*e long for work that is meaningful and significant, work that* brings us joy. We long to know that the work of our hands and our minds is good—that in word and deed we are doing something fundamentally positive and worthwhile.

Thomas Merton ably describes the lack of true and good work, work that has lost its vitality:

> Unnatural, frantic, anxious work, work done under pressure of greed or fear or any other inordinate passion, cannot properly speaking be dedicated to God, because God never wills such work directly. He may permit that, through no fault of our own, we may have to work madly and distractedly, due to our sins, and to the sins of the society in which we live. In that case we must tolerate it and make the best of what we cannot avoid. But let us not be blind to the distinction between sound, healthy work and unnatural toil.[1]

Merton's statement reminds us that we long for two things. First, we long for work that is meaningful and rewarding, work that we enjoy and in which we feel we are doing something significant and valuable. We long to know that we are making a difference.

But further, we long to know that our work brings pleasure to God and has his blessing. That is, we want to have work that is meaningful and rewarding for our own sake, but we also want that work to be something that we do for God.

Two texts of Holy Scripture capture this in phrases that are worth keeping in mind. The first is Ecclesiastes 2:24. "There is nothing better for mortals than to . . . find enjoyment in their toil. This also, I saw, is from the hand of God." God gives us work as a gift, and we find joy and satisfaction in it.

The second reference is in Colossians. "Whatever your task, put yourselves into it, as done for the Lord and not for your masters" (Col 3:23; see also Eph 6:5-8). While St. Paul was writing this to people who were slaves, the principle is applicable to all regardless of the work to which we are called.

The fundamental features of vocational integrity are simple. They are captured in the two principles outlined in chapter two: know yourself and be true to who you are. But more is required in order to flesh out what it means to have integrity in our activity in the world—in our work, our career and our vocation. It is this "more" that enables us to work with joy and satisfaction.

For this, we first need to know that what we are doing comes from God; we can take joy and pleasure in our work or responsibilities because they are given to us by God. Whether it is the task of raising children, of running a business, of providing pastoral leadership for a church or of teaching a Sunday school class, it is from the Lord. Second, we need to have a sense that what we are doing is done "as to the Lord" (Col 3:23 KJV). It is something we do with a Godward orientation—something that we offer back to God. In other words, our work is both given to us by God and offered back to God.

It has been my impression for some time that three of the epistles of Paul are essentially calls for vocational integrity: 1 and 2 Timothy and Titus. This is particularly the case with 2 Timothy. The elder apostle writes to Timothy challenging him to fulfill his call and to do so with diligence, focus and courage. While Timothy's was a specifically religious vocation, it is not difficult to draw from Paul's words the qualities and characteristics that have immediate application to all of us, regardless of call or vocation. Paul describes in this letter what it means to do our work with joy and satisfaction because we do it as something we have *from* the hand of God and something that we do as *to* the Lord.

Paul emphasizes four qualities, each of which he clearly considers essential if Timothy and others are to have vocational integrity, and these qualities are captured in four words: *excellence, truth, diligence* and *generosity*. Each of these is an antidote to what Merton calls "unnatural toil."

To these four qualities I would add a fifth element that stands alone and provides the context in which we are able to do work that is characterized by excellence, truth, diligence and generosity. This fifth element, sabbath rest, is critical for a simple reason: each of the other four can be embraced and pursued to a fault. The pursuit of excellence can become perfectionism; the pursuit of truth, bigotry; and the pursuit of diligence, hectic activity. Even generosity can be misguided. We must call one another to pursue these qualities in a manner that is life-giving rather than pursuing them to a fault, which is deathly. This fifth element, sabbath rest, then, makes all the difference.

Excellence

First the apostle says to Timothy: "Do your *best* to present yourself to God as . . . a worker who has no need to be ashamed, rightly explaining the word of truth" (2 Tim 2:15). Paul is reaffirming a vital principle of the spiritual life: that we are given gifts and capacities and that to be true to ourselves we must exercise them to the *best* of our ability.

The Bible assumes a fundamental commitment to excellence. But there is an important element to this biblical assumption that must not be overlooked, and it is this: Excellence is ultimately judged by whether or not we did *our* best. If we have ten talents, we are judged differently than a person with four talents. We are judged according to our distinctive circumstances, opportunities, education and ability. Excellence is found in fulfilling your vocation in the service of truth to the very best of *your* ability, with a continued commitment to serve God as well as *you* are able. We are not judged by some arbitrary or contrived standard.

Having said that, within each discipline or craft or occupation, there is a distinct sense of what is good and what is minimally adequate. When my teeth are being repaired, I relax in the dentist's chair because I know that a master is hovering over me and is diligently at work on my molars. And I will accept nothing less than the very best work; they are my teeth, after all. If my dentist calmly but sincerely informs me that he has bungled things up, his sincerity counts for nothing; he is liable for malpractice.

But within the minimal standards of what is good within each craft or occupation, we are ultimately accountable for doing our work to the very best of our ability, and we should not be satisfied with anything less than our best.

Our only hope for excellence, over the long haul, is to capture what the apostle Paul addresses in Colossians 3:23: that we do our work "as to the Lord" rather than for human masters or employers. In other words, our criteria for excellence is whether we can confidently say before God that we have done our best. Because in the end it is only God who knows if it was. Some people have a remarkable ability to "wing it," whether it is in academic work, in selling a product or in public speaking. Because of their facility they are not pressed to prepare carefully or do background research. Inevitably, though, it all catches up with them; the quality of their work begins to fade, and the initial aura of excellence is lost.

In the end, only you and God know if you did your best. If we do our work "as to the Lord," then we will do our best regardless of what others say or think. I do not know what good dental work looks like; I just want pain-free chewing! But I delight in knowing that my dentist takes pride in his work quite apart from whether I appreciate the care he has taken in his craft.

As noted above, each of these four qualities can be embraced to a fault. We must distinguish between the love and pursuit of excellence on the one hand and perfectionism on the other. Perfectionism is a misguided pursuit of excellence. A genuine love of excellence is rooted in the conviction that God deserves our best and that other people deserve nothing less. But the perfectionist is self-centered; excellence has become an end in itself. Perfectionists are always dissatisfied—with themselves and with others. Their work is never a joy because it is never good enough. *They* are never good enough. Rather than delighting in work well done for the sake of others, they are consumed with themselves and their own performance. Rather than working joyfully with others, they are demanding and uncompromising, incapable of accepting the miscues of others.

The genuine love of excellence is rooted in a desire to serve well. Because our work comes from the hand of God, we offer it back to God as our act of thankful worship.

Truth

Good and rewarding work, work that is done "as to the Lord," is offered in the service of truth; it is truthful—full of truth.

When the apostle Paul writes to Timothy, he calls him to a ministry of truth—in word and deed—that for him comes through particularly in his call to preach and teach. In the same verse in which Paul urges Timothy to "do his best," he adds another qualifier—he should do his best in the service of truth, specifically the noble task of "explaining the word of truth" (2 Tim 2:15).

Timothy was called to be a teacher and a preacher of truth. The apostle Paul addresses this when he writes of his own calling. He insists that he is not a "peddler" of God's word. Rather "we refuse to practice cunning or to falsify God's word; but by the open statement of truth we commend ourselves to the conscience of everyone in the sight of God" (2 Cor 2:17; see also 4:2).

The same principle applies to all who make their living through speaking—to teachers, politicians or counselors. If we are nothing more than peddlers, speaking in a manner that is self-serving rather than truth-serving, we clearly violate something that is at the heart of who it is we are called to be.

But this call to truth is not unique to those whose vocation requires speaking. All authentic vocations are focused on truth. My wife is an artist; she has vocational integrity only when her work is full of truth. The same applies to a novelist, a business person, an advertiser, a lawyer, a doctor.

Even if we have embraced our rightful vocation we do so falsely if we use our vocation for selfish ends or at the service of that which is false. When an engineer accepts that a building structure is deeply flawed and when a business person sells a product that he knows is shoddily crafted, they violate what it means to work with integrity. They turn work on its head, making it self-serving rather than others-serving. Integrity requires a fundamental honesty—with our customers or clients, our employees and our stockholders. It demands honesty with the children we are raising.

A carpenter who works with wood and a landscaper who designs the spaces around buildings are both working with God-given materials, and they have the opportunity to work with integrity, in the service of the truth, or to do work that is shoddy, artificial and contrived.

Vocational integrity is found only when we focus on and serve truth; and this arises, of course, from a fundamental loyalty *to* truth. But here also, I urge caution. It might be hard to conceive of someone serving truth to a fault—in a way that is excessive. But consider this: is there not something wrong with the fundamentalist whose supposed commitment to truth negates all other perspectives or points of view? And when I speak of a fundamentalist, I have in mind the religious bigot, the ultraradical feminist or the nationalist. Something is askew when our passion for truth blinds us to other perspectives and prevents us from disagreeing graciously and learning from others who see things differently than we do.

Sometimes people get locked on a principle or a conviction that represents one dimension of the truth, and they become crusaders for that perspective. The conviction may be a true one, but it becomes deadly in the hands of a zealot. A genuine love of truth is always complemented by the humility evident in a gracious, teachable spirit. We must be wary particularly of those who, as the apostle Paul puts it, get caught up in argumentation and debate, consumed with "wrangling over words, which does no good" (2 Tim 2:14). Paul calls Timothy to the service of truth, but he also urges him to avoid those who are quarrelsome, and to do his work with gentleness, kindness and patience (2:23-25).

There is yet another way in which truth intersects with vocation. We are only full of truth in our vocation if we are true to our word. People of integrity are those who do what they say they will do and who live their lives in a manner that is consistent with their professed values. These include preachers who call us to walk in the light, teachers whose lives and actions speak more loudly than the content of their lectures, politicians whose commitment to fundamental values ultimately determines the quality of their leadership, and engineers who understand and work with the integrity of a material and its capacity to do what it has been designed to do.

Diligence

Alongside excellence and truthfulness we must consider another virtue. The call to diligence appears often in the apostle Paul's letters to Timothy and Titus, especially at the high point of his second letter to Timothy, when he urges him to proclaim the message and to be *persistent* in this task (2 Tim 4:2).

Diligence involves *persistence*. Timothy is urged to persevere in his work "whether the time is favorable or unfavorable; . . . with the utmost patience." Diligence involves doing our work with a care and commitment that does not waver depending on the level of affirmation we are getting on a particular day. We do what we do because it needs to be done.

More than that, diligence involves what Paul speaks of later in the same chapter when he calls Timothy to "carry out your ministry fully" (2 Tim 4:5). Diligence includes *thoroughness*. There is no substitute for hard work. I am increasingly convinced that there is no task that is easy in itself. For an athlete to compete well, hard work is involved—regardless of how gifted or talented the athlete happens to be. And much of that hard work happens behind the scenes—in a rigorous fitness program that continues day in and day out far from the eyes of sports fans. Similarly, musicians can only become accomplished at their task if they practice with a thoroughness and persistence that in itself receives little reward or affirmation.

The same principle applies to all of us. People who work in administration know that a great deal of the work that needs to be done just has to be done—whether anyone notices or particularly cares. Attention to detail must be a personal commitment or it is not a commitment at all. We must learn to enjoy the satisfaction of a job done well, to enjoy our work so that there is satisfaction in the quality of the work itself rather than in the gratitude or approval of others.

In our work there is no easy way. We must watch out for the patterns of "corner cutting." It is not that we should labor over details for the sake of details; rather we must have a commitment to persist and to do our work completely—with care and diligence.

But do not confuse diligence and hard work with hectic activity or over-work. Many people are consumed by work and by all the things they think need to be done. Like the perfectionist, they are never satisfied. As Merton puts it, their toil is "frantic, anxious work." The antidote to laziness is not hectic activity. Ironically, when we are consumed by hectic activity, we are essentially doing our work and that of others, which means that we are not doing our own work well—with care, diligence and grace.

Of course there will be seasons of our lives and our work when we live under the intensity of the moment or the season. Athletes press to prepare for a big event; professors spend long hours at the end of the term complet-ing their grading; businesspeople stay late in order to have the shop ready for a special promotion the next day. But it is when we come to live habitu-ally in this way that we know something is askew; our lives and work reflect empty busyness, not true diligence.

Generosity

Fourth, it is imperative that we affirm the integrity of our work and the ful-fillment of our vocation by doing what we do with *generosity*. In 2 Corin-thians 5:16 the apostle Paul reminds his readers that by virtue of the work of Christ we no longer consider others in purely human categories; rather we see them as new creations. We see them with hope and potential; we see every human being as having incomparable worth and significance. It is this conviction that lies behind Paul's insistence that we live for others, in generous service.

There is a difference between *generous* service and *calculated* service. Calculated service counts the cost and considers the return, reward or pay-ment. Generous service is given freely—one person giving for the sake of another. It is not given even for the thanks that one might receive; it is given freely and with generosity. Simone Weil says of *true* service that it "is as instinctive and immediate as it is for oneself to eat when one is hungry," and "it is forgotten almost at once, just as one forgets yesterday's meals."[2]

In fact, our service is *for another*. We serve Christ in response to his love, and we serve others in his name. We can give freely within our family, to our friends, within our congregation and in the world. Indeed, it is probably critical that we see our work—whatever form it takes—as something that we do for God and not for others. Though we may be paid for our work, and though that payment is necessary for us to meet our financial needs, our service does not need to be calculated. I may get paid to teach in the public school, but I can see myself as being there in the name of Christ to serve the children in my classroom, and to work generously with my colleagues. We must beware of the subtle temptation to calculate service given. Generous service is not rendered in order to procure a secondary or indirect result, to win a following or to gain the cooperation or loyalty of another.

Further, generous service empowers those we serve. False forms of service create dependence; true service, given in love, enables another to grow, mature, stand alone and eventually give, as we serve one another in interdependence. In true service there is always giving and receiving. A hospital nurse may recognize that he is also the recipient when he serves a patient, and he remains open to the subtle and joyous ways in which patients can give to him. I do not mean that we serve for the thanks and recognition we will receive but rather that we need the other, the very one we serve. Pastors can consciously live in the recognition that they are served by their parishioners—not because the parishioners are contributors to the pastor's projects but because they give and receive interdependently.

An important and necessary qualifier needs to be added here. Just as God has not gifted us to do everything, even so we are not called to be or do everything for everyone who comes our way. Parker Palmer notes that though God loves everyone, I am not called to be the means by which everyone knows and experiences his love.[3] We do not have supernatural strength or stamina; we are limited beings. Moreover, we must have priorities. There are times when my generosity with others undercuts my capacity to be genuinely present and generous with my wife and my children. It is simply not possible to be generous at all times and in all places with all people; we have limited time and energy.

Those who try to be all things to all people, those who sacrifice fundamental relationships—such as with spouse and children—because they are consumed with their work in the world are perhaps generous, but theirs is a misguided generosity. It is so easy to fall into the trap of being very solicitous toward others but neglecting our own family. With misguided generosity people usually seek to be more than God is calling them to be and do more than God is calling them to do. Often what drives such people is a longing to be affirmed and appreciated. Their work is not tied directly to their call. For God does not call us to do more than can be done within the actual context of our lives and relationships.

Whenever we are consumed with work, busy with hectic activity, it is imperative that we back away and prayerfully discern our calling, clarifying what it is that God is calling us to be and do—with generosity—in this place and at this time. We cannot fulfill our vocation well if we are physically and emotionally drained, or if we are impatient and tired and frustrated with people. Part of true service is learning the simple art of saying no, of recognizing our priorities and our limitations.

Sabbath

Excellence, truth, diligence and generosity. These are the qualities that make our work enjoyable and satisfying, as something that we have from the hand of God. They are also the indicators that we are resolved to do our work "as to the Lord."

Each of these can be life; but each can also be death. When any of these qualities is pursued as an end in itself, it has a shadow side that makes work hell. The pursuit of excellence becomes the burden of perfectionism—a burden to you and to those with whom you work. The pursuit of truth becomes bigotry—a misguided and one-dimensional zeal for a single, exclusive dimension of truth. The pursuit of diligence can become nothing more than hectic activity that leaves us overworked and exhausted, not a servant to the community but a burden to self and others. And confused generosity leaves us overcommitted, eager to give but without a sense of purpose or focus to our giving, lacking reasonable constraints.

What can enable us to pursue each of these qualities as life-giving objectives? What can keep us from the shadow side of each of them?

Our only hope is to keep a balance—a balance that comes with sustaining whole, integrated lives. We must be people of work and leisure, persons of prayer and work, women and men who are called to both worship and service.

We must remember that our work is never the whole of who we are; we can never be defined purely as "workers." Yes, we are persons who have work to do; but we are always more than workers. Our work is never the sum and total of who we are. Even though our work is important to us, rarely is it the most important thing about us.

We must sustain a clear sense of the relational dimension of our lives—that we are spouses, parents and friends, who live and love as members of communities.

All of this is only possible with a clearly defined pattern of sabbath renewal in our lives. The ancient Hebrew people observed the Sabbath with great care as a day of rest. This day gave perspective to the whole of their lives, particularly to their work. It was a weekly reminder that their ultimate identity was not wrapped up in their work; they belonged to God.

Through observance of the Sabbath the Hebrew people affirmed that their livelihood was the means by which the Lord cared for their basic human needs, and through observance of the Sabbath they sustained the perspective that ultimately it is the Lord who provides. The Sabbath was also a means to experience necessary rest, a re-creation, an enjoyment of God's creation and of one another.

Regular sabbath rest frees me from seeing my work as a burden. The work that is entrusted to me for six days a week is ultimately God's work, but I am not responsible to feel the burden of carrying it seven days a week. The sabbath thus gives perspective.

In our urbanized world, where medical staff, pastors, police officers and many others need to work on Sundays, it is imperative that we recognize that the principle of sabbath rest applies to all, whether or not everyone observes the same day of the week. Sabbath rest is not so much a day off as it is a day when we rest from our work and re-create—in worship, leisure, prayer and fellowship, all with a view toward delighting in God, his creation and others, particularly family and friends. We should not even call it a day off for then we are defining our sabbath rest negatively in terms of the absence of work. The sabbath rest is meaningful in its own right. We are called to it just as we are called to work, and we enjoy it because we love God and others.

Futhermore, each day can, and perhaps should, include a form of sabbath rest, a time of quiet. For some people this time will fall in the early morning; for others it will come at midday when they step away from the workplace and find a quiet church sanctuary for a few minutes of silence and meditation.

Each type of sabbath rest—one day in seven, or a few minutes of silence in every day—is a way in which we step back from and find perspective for our work.

Conclusion

In the face of the challenges and opportunities that Timothy faced, the apostle Paul was not asking him to be a hero or a miracle worker but merely to remain true to his vocation.

The same applies to us. We may see the tremendous needs of our world, and we may be tempted to be heroes, charging off to save the world. But we are called back to vocational clarity and commitment—to fulfilling what we have been called to do in the service of truth.

At times our vocation is undermined because of pride. We are unwilling to accept what God has given us because we do not want to accept some aspect of our calling that appears to lack the prestige, status or remuneration we want or believe we deserve. And we can easily get caught in the trap of looking ahead—doing what we are doing so that we will noticed, so that we will be promoted, so that we will obtain another job, perhaps. And the consequence is that we are consumed with ourselves, and no longer honest about our limitations, our priorities, our calling—our selves. The longer we live such a lie the sooner it will be that we are nothing more than hollow people.

Our only hope is to intentionally embrace the call of God. This is joy, a joy that will sustain us and give life to those with whom we live and work. There is great joy in knowing what God has called us to be and do, and in acting with courage and humility in response to a needy world. Joy is found in giving ourselves fully—eagerly and passionately—to our call.

For this joyful life, though, we must learn to *think* vocationally. And to that premise we now turn.

Five

THINKING
VOCATIONALLY

*D*avid Bosch, in his very fine exposition of 2 Corinthians, *Spirituality of the Road,* describes what he sees as a typical crisis for missionaries.[1] His insights are equally applicable to all of us, regardless of our calling. He notes that missionaries in mid-career face two dangers or temptations. Some are tempted by busyness. They become wrapped up in hectic activity, consumed with running from one thing to another. Their days are so full that they have lost the capacity to live with serenity. They are exhausted and, as often as not, confused. They are sincere in their desire to serve, but their generosity has left them overextended. The danger is that they are little more than harried workers.

For many people hectic activity provides a kind of perpetual adrenaline rush. Often those who are consumed by busyness feel that this pattern of life and work legitimates them. They feel important; they feel needed; they feel alive. But it is a false sense of life and importance, and eventually it leaves them feeling hollow.

The second pattern that Bosch identifies is the temptation to laxity. Rather than having a busy and hectic lifestyle, some people fall into a pattern of puttering about, going through the motions, accomplishing little if anything. They have lost a sense of purpose and focus; they are no longer genuinely engaged with their lives and their work. In some cases they are overwhelmed by the needs around them and do not know where to begin. In other cases, either they are slothful or they lack passion. They have become apathetic and have lost a desire for work, and there is little if any joy in their service.

Both of these are temptations because they call us away from who we truly are, what we are fundamentally called to be and do. They draw us away from life. Whatever the reasons for falling into one or the other of these temptations, the fact is that something is askew in either case.

If we are beset by either temptation, the way forward is to think vocationally.

The Advantages of Thinking Vocationally

The advantages of thinking vocationally are many, and each is a variation on the theme of freedom from the burden of pretense, freedom to be who we are truly called to be. Ultimately this freedom is expressed in joy. Each of the benefits, in its own way, leads to joyful freedom—the freedom and joy of people who know who they are called to be and have the courage and capacity to embrace their vocation.

We are freed from comparing ourselves to one another. To think vocationally means to make an appraisal of the self. We look at ourselves; we identify, accept and embrace who we are called to be. This focus on ourselves frees us from comparing ourselves to others. And this liberates. For when we refuse to compare ourselves to one another, when we reject envy and jealousy of others, of their gifts and abilities and opportunities, we are freed to be who *we* are. The giftedness of another person is not a threat to us. As James Fowler writes: "In vocation we are augmented by others' talents rather than being diminished or threatened by them."[2]

Comparing ourselves to others is a real problem in a time of massive amounts of television exposure. The television elevates the gifts of some people, making them stars whose influence, glamour and style can easily discourage people who think they could never be a star. Why should I teach an adult Bible study class, someone might wonder, when everyone has the option of watching and listening to a famous teacher on video? The pressure makes some people think that if they cannot be a star they might as well not be anything.

But a true sense of vocation is rooted in the reality that there is something that we *must* do, even if it means we will never be famous. You are faithful to *your* vocation, ultimately, because you resolve to be true to *yourself,* for only then can you be true to your God.

If we are freed from comparisons, we are also freed from competition. We can reject the notion that to fulfill our vocation we must get ahead of others so their development or success will not limit us. We can genuinely celebrate the accomplishments of others without fear that their achievements somehow diminish us.

We are freed from artificial standards of excellence. When we view our life and our work through the lens of vocation, we are called to an excellence based not on competition but rather on being true to ourselves and to our own potential. Then the challenge of doing our work with excellence is not a burden; rather it is something that frees us—frees us to exercise our gifts and talents without fear of failure. Failure is just part of the learning process; it need not diminish us.

Because there is no contrived or burdensome notion of excellence, we are also free to accept our limitations just as we accept our potential. Our limitations—our areas of non-strength or the things we do not do well—can be accepted with grace and humility. We do not need to feel diminished by them.

Only as we embrace a standard of excellence that is not imposed artificially, but fits who we are, can we move into emotional maturity in our capacity to think vocationally. It is said that Martin Luther King Jr. sought a particular freedom, an emotional freedom from two things: an inflated head when praised and a crushed spirit when criticized. Both affirmation and criticism will come our way. Sometimes our work will be praised, and sometimes our work will be deemed inadequate. Indeed, both praise and criticism will come more than once! And we need both. Affirmation and criticism are essential to our development and to the process of discernment. We need the encouragement of affirmation; we need the discipline, the accountability and the checking of our aspirations that come with criticism. But both affirmation and criticism can derail us emotionally if we are not careful.

Our commitment to excellence, when it is understood in terms of our vocation and in light of our own capabilities, frees us so that we can hear *both* affirmation and criticism with grace. We will not be flattered by praise, and our spirits will not be crushed by criticism. This is an essential posture from which we are able to live and work with freedom and joy.

We are freed from the burden of pleasing everyone. With this understanding of vocation, we are freed from the burden of needing to be liked by everyone and of trying to please everyone.

To please everyone is simply not possible; to try to is a burden that we cannot possibly bear. When we are trapped in the need to please everyone, we are soon confronted with critical matters of integrity. Even if they try always to please others and their underlying passion is being liked by everyone, politicians will never be able to meet the demands of every constituent; administrators will never satisfy each member of the organization; and a parent will simply never be able to provide everything his or her child desires. It is not possible.

Not only is the need to please burdensome, it also usually leads to a lie. We end up living according to the expectations of others and what they want us to be and do. Some of us manage to live this way for a remarkably long period of time. We are like chameleons, and we are able to make the people we are with believe that we have their best interests in mind. We are able to parrot what we think people want to hear. But inevitably this becomes a lie. When it comes to tough decisions—whether in the home or at work—we end up trying to cut it both ways. It is an impossible burden.

We are freed from urgency and the tyranny of time. When we think vocationally, we are freed from the oppressive burden of trying to get as much done as possible. We are freed from trying to do too much or from doing work merely to try to legitimate ourselves or to show our worth. We are freed from hectic work-for-work's-sake; we can give our time and energy knowing that there is plenty of time in any given day to do what we are called to do. And, as James Fowler notes, when we are freed from the burden of trying to do as much as possible, from the tyranny of time, then "time is our friend rather than our enemy."[3]

When we think vocationally, we are freed to enjoy times of worship, play and leisure without worrying that we should be working, accomplishing something, getting something done before a pressing deadline. Whatever God is calling us to do now, at this point in our lives, can be done within the limitations of our current life situation. God rarely, if ever, calls us to be or to do so much that we must sacrifice the fundamental relationships of our lives or neglect our need for sleep, rest, friendship, worship and recreation. Thinking vocationally frees us from the burden of a perpetual sense of urgency.

We are freed to love others. In Romans 12:3, Paul calls us to look at ourselves with sober judgement—to think truthfully and honestly about who we are. Then he calls us to love one another, and specifically to "let love be genuine" (Rom 12:9). I am convinced that there is an underlying logic to the progression of Paul's thought at this point: that we can only truly love another, without hypocrisy, when we think vocationally, when we truly and graciously identify, accept and embrace who *we* are.

Any other posture is burdensome; it cannot lead to genuine love. Sometimes our generosity is misguided and our love for others is offered out of a busy and hectic spirit rather than out of serenity and joy. Sometimes we are caught up in the desire to be loved and in the hope that everyone will like us, and this inevitably undermines our capacity to love genuinely.

When we think vocationally, we are freed from what A. W. Tozer calls the burden of pretense and enter into the freedom of humility. Tozer reminds us of the joy that comes when we are freed of artificiality, of the burden of trying to impress others.[4] When we recover the principle of vocation, we are able to embrace authenticity, genuineness and truthfulness. This is freedom; and it is a freedom to love others authentically.

Obstacles to Vocation

There are benefits of thinking vocationally, and there are also obstacles that undermine our capacity to think vocationally. While the obstacles are different for different people, most, if not all of us, will encounter certain commonalities that impede our capacity to discern and embrace our call. In most cases they are burdens that weigh us down.

A sacred-secular distinction in the understanding of vocation. One obstacle to vocational identity and fulfillment is essentially theological—the failure to appreciate the sacredness of all vocations. This sacred-secular split reflects a particular understanding of how God operates in the world. When we deny that all vocations are sacred, we become caught in one of two traps or burdens. The first burden is that we accept a vocation that is not fundamentally our own. We go into the pastorate or become a missionary because we think this is a more noble way. It is a burden and a heavy weight because it is not our personal call. We accept a role because we think we should, but we cannot experience the joyful abandon of those who know they are doing what God is calling them to do. Inevitably, when this happens we feel the burden ourselves, but we are also a burden to those around us. Our lack of joy can only mean that we are not living and working in harmony with others, for we are not in harmony with ourselves.

Others of us may not have become missionaries or pastors, but we feel as though we *should* have done so. If we feel this way even if the full-time gospel ministry is not our calling, then we have fallen into the second trap: we have not eagerly embraced what it is that God truly is calling us to. Thus farmers and business people, rather than celebrating and embracing their call, are apologetic about the work they do and view it as far from the ideal of what a Christian should be doing. And one common outcome is that they then pressure their children into religious work as a way of compensating for their own failure to be "all that God wanted them to be."

This pattern of defining what is truly "sacred" happens in more subtle ways in different work settings. I was amazed to discover that among missionaries in the Philippines there was an implied hierarchy: the "real" missionaries were doing evangelism and church planting while the "quasi" missionaries were doing administration or relief and development. In the academic world there is a remarkable inclination to celebrate the research scholar and not to recognize the sacredness of every role that is critical to making a college or university effective.

When we fail to affirm the sacredness of all vocations, we create burdens for people—the burden of assuming a role or responsibility that is not truly their own and the burden of not embracing the work that God has indeed called them to. Again, in both of these cases people not only carry an unnecessary burden, but they become a burden to others.

Failure to distinguish between vocation and career or occupation. For other people, a major obstacle to vocational fulfillment is the failure to distinguish between vocation and role or career. Their vocation, as they understand it, relates to a very particular situation—perhaps a particular role or occupation. I remember hearing a young missionary say that he was called to the Philippines for life. I was amazed both at the audacity of such a suggestion (there was always the chance the Filipino people would not want him there for life), and at the limitation that his certainty imposed. God is not capricious, but if we are going to think vocationally we must be more flexible. We must not tie our sense of vocation to a particular place or role.

After all, we could be dismissed from the company or organization where we work. But that does not mean that we would lose our vocation. I know of some pastors' wives who cannot think of themselves other than as a kind of auxiliary to their husbands. They will have a crisis of identity and call if their husband chooses to leave pastoral ministry. And quite apart from that possibility, they have so linked their sense of call to a particular kind of role or responsibility that they undermine their own capacity to truly think vocationally.

Whether we have identified our sense of vocation with a particular company or organization or whether we have overidentified ourselves with the vocation or occupation of a spouse, we are undercutting our capacity to take responsibility for our own life and vocation. I am not questioning the value of commitment to our spouse or to a church or organization. I value highly my coworkers who demonstrate a deep commitment to our organization and who are prepared to live out their days in eager service there. But something is askew when we cannot imagine being anywhere else and when our whole lives are consequently wrapped up in a particular organization or role.

It is a noble desire to support and encourage our spouse, even to identify eagerly with our spouse's calling. But when one spouse has a crisis of identity when the other's inevitable job change comes, the ironic truth becomes clear: the commitment was actually to the auxiliary role rather than to the spouse. We set ourselves up for vocational crisis when we identify ourselves too closely with either an organization or a person; for we may be lost at sea when inevitable changes come.

Organizations will change. They must, not merely to survive, but also to respond effectively to new opportunities and circumstances. Those who are overly identified with an organization and cannot imagine that they would work anywhere else find that they are constantly on the defensive, doing all they can to resist the changes that are necessary for the well-being of the organization. They are not really committed to the organization; they are committed to what the organization used to be or to what they hope it will continue to be.

The three classic temptations. It is probably safe to say that the greatest threats to vocational thinking are three classic temptations. They are essentially the temptations that Jesus faced in the desert at the beginning of his public life and ministry (Lk 4:1-13): the desire for *power*, the desire for *material security* and comfort, and the desire for fame or *prestige*. It is easy to make vocational choices that are rooted in or motivated by these powerful and subtle temptations; it is then easy to rationalize choices around each of them. But these temptations have an insidious effect on a vocation.

How many of us have rationalized away what God is calling us to do because we cannot bear the thought of a drop in our standard of living or the threat of financial insecurity? How many of us have chosen a line of work simply because it seems to guarantee a healthy pension and thus a comfortable retirement? Many of us have gotten ourselves into debt or financial obligations that severely thwart our capacity to embrace what God is calling us to be. Money is not evil, but the desire for material well-being and security has driven many of us to live in a way that is inconsistent with our vocation.

Some of us are driven by different agendas. In my religious community so much praise and prestige is focused on the religious vocation that many people have become and remained missionaries largely because of the praise and uncritical affirmation that they get from a community that has viewed the missionary call as the premier and most sacred call, somehow above evaluation and critique.

I remember a student in a course I taught on vocation. He spoke of a missionary convention where, at age thirteen, he was praised and brought up to the front of the church to be prayed for when he indicated that he was willing to be a missionary. As a young man he looked back on the event and noted that it was too much praise and affirmation for a thirteen-year-old. Not only did it feed his ego at the time, but as he grew older it profoundly undermined his capacity to think critically and with discernment about his call.

Some people may hear the young man's story and suggest that he needs to be faithful to the call that he received at age thirteen. In fact, what we must learn to do as Christian communities is to trust the call of God on each life, affirming and encouraging individuals to accept *whatever* it is that God is calling them to do rather than prodding and pigeonholing them onto a particular path.

Many times I catch myself doing things or accepting invitations to speak or teach largely because I desire to be noticed. Something deep inside me fears obscurity. But I know that the desire to be noticed is death to my vocation. Most of what we are called to do will only be fulfilled if we let go of the desire for praise, affirmation and prestige. Failure to do so will eventually catch up with us; eventually we will become hollow people.

Others of us set aside or suppress our true vocation because of the temptation of power. It is always sad to see people accept positions of supposed influence because they are drawn to what they perceive as the power that accompanies those positions, people who move into administration or management when they are really called to something else. Personally, I had to repeatedly ask and confirm whether academic administration was indeed my calling. But when I was a missionary I noticed, especially among men, the temptation reflected in the desire to be elected to serve on the governing executive committee or to be field director. As young men we would long for these positions whether or not they truly reflected our fundamental call and identity, and apparently we were not concerned about whether such an election would keep us from our calling.

When we accept or pursue positions, roles or occupations because we long for material plenty, prestige or power, it is because we hope to fill an emotional vacuum, a deep and perhaps legitimate longing that we hope will be fulfilled with money, power or fame. For example, I often hear of men who are doing what they are doing in their occupations because they never received the approval they needed from their fathers, and now, through this other avenue, hope to find it.

In view of this, one of the most fruitful and necessary exercises in vocational thinking is to think critically about our motives, to probe into what it really is that leads us to do what we think we must do. Only as we are honest about our motives can we even begin to discern vocation well.

Misguided sense of duty. A misguided sense of duty is also an obstacle to vocational fulfillment. It manifests itself in a variety of ways.

Parker Palmer speaks, for example, of people who feel obligated to acquire an education or to invest time and money into a training program.[5] The pressure they feel may come from their own sense of duty or from people who helped pay for their education, expecting that a specific career will reflect their training and help pay off the bills.

The problem is twofold. First, many people enter into costly educational programs before they are able to discern their true identity and calling. Second, if people spend an inordinate amount of money to study medicine they may have the unfortunate idea that the money will be wasted if they do not become doctors.

What we consider "wasted" is always relative. Isn't it much worse for people to waste their vocation, to remain in the field of medicine out of a sense of duty because they have a medical degree, when they know, deep in their gut, that medicine does not reflect their true calling?

Concern about wasted education also reflects a narrow understanding of how God works in our lives. With God there is no wasted time. We will be surprised by how the threads of our lives are woven together, how they unfold in the tapestry that God is creating in us and through us. We cannot always see how things are working themselves out. All we can do is choose, for now, for *this* day, to be true to who we are and who we are called to be. No education, however wonderful or expensive, should undermine our capacity to think clearly about that call.

A misguided sense of duty is exposed in another way when we confuse compliance with the important and legitimate discipline of spiritual submission. We are called to live in submission within Christian community. We cannot function effectively within the organizations in which we work if we do not acknowledge and live out of the reality that someone must have authority and will probably make decisions with which we disagree.

Compliance is another matter. When people in authority call for compliance, they are calling for unthinking, undiscerning obedience. Many religious leaders want this, implying that anyone who differs with them is disloyal, either to them or to the church. They believe that compliance and submission are one and the same.

We are called to accountability and submission; we are called to live in gracious harmony within the Christian community and this means that we need to let leaders lead. But we must never equate the voice of leadership with the voice of God. We must always distinguish between the prompting of the Spirit on the one hand, and the voice of human authorities on the other. Our fundamental posture must be one of submission and honor; but we must live and work with the understanding that the voice of God and the voice of those in authority over us are not necessarily the same.

A misguided sense of duty also undercuts our capacity to fulfill our vocation when we act on the fear that someone will be threatened by us. We hesitate to act and embrace an opportunity—and perhaps even our calling—because we do not want to do anything that might make another person feel diminished. If people feel diminished by our success it is really *their* problem, but we take it on as our burden. Some married people do not want be a threat to their spouses, some friends do not want to outshine their peers, and some employees do not want to threaten their supervisors.

While it is imperative that we live with sensitivity to the emotional well-being of others, we cannot afford to be straitjacketed by their emotional immaturity. We owe it to them as well as to God and to ourselves to "fan into flame" the gifts and opportunities that God has given us. We are accountable for our stewardship of those gifts. And ultimately we are not doing others a favor when we protect them from their own emotional insecurities. All we are doing is hurting ourselves.

We also have a misguided sense of duty when we stay with an organization or a job long after we should have resigned. We have made duty our highest value. Some of us have so equated our identity with a company or an organization that we sustain an inappropriate level of loyalty to it. The consequence is a disconnection from our vocation. Rarely is an individual called to make a life-long covenant commitment to a company, a school, a religious organization or a movement. Rarely. In most cases God calls us to hold lightly to our institutional commitments—to serve eagerly with others but also to recognize that God will sometimes call us to leave. We should not be capricious in our commitments, but neither should we overstay when God calls us to move on.[6]

Maturity is found when we resolve that we will be true to who we are called to be, that we will not live by imitation of others, or by compliance or conformity to others' ideals for us. If we have an appropriate sense of duty, it will be reflected in our resolve to be faithful to who we are and who we have been called to be.

Failing to appreciate our limits. There are two other major obstacles to vocational thinking, which at first may not seem related but which have one common feature—the failure to understand the meaning of limits in our lives and our work.

Some people seem to think about nothing but their limits. They tend to overstate the boundaries or limitations of their lives and their work. And others, at the opposite end of the pole, fail to see any limits at all.

People in the first group are usually inclined, for whatever reason, to feel victimized. They blame others for the limitations they are feeling. They may blame their parents or their previous employers or their colleagues or their current employer. Rather than taking responsibility for their own sphere of life and for their own actions and reactions, they blame others. Their feeling of victimization is a straitjacket. And they speak of themselves as though they are martyrs.

At the other end of the pole are those who see no limits. They are the heroes, those who, with messianic idealism, see themselves as doing great and noble things for God, often for religious causes. And they are inclined to call others to be great heroes in their work for God as well. Deep within American culture is a viewpoint that has affected so many in the West, the idea that anyone who has the will and determination can be anything they want to be and do anything they want to do. It is merely a matter of hard work and determination. But this is a false perspective. It is simply not true. What truth there is in this notion lies in the value of hard work. But it is not true that we are all called to be heroes doing great and grandiose things for God.

The problem is simple: God often calls people to the obscure, the ordinary and the mundane. He accomplishes some of his most important work in the world through ordinary people doing ordinary things. We should not merely tolerate this ordinariness; rather we must embrace and even celebrate it. Some of us miss our vocation because we are looking for the heroic. We fail to accept the limitations of life and the fact that God's work through us is often in the small and the ordinary. We also fail to realize that the work we are called to do will often be very difficult and that things we accomplish will happen slowly and incrementally. We are not heroes; we are merely people who are doing our best in our day-to-day work.

The genius of truth and freedom is found in accepting our limitations without overstating their significance. It is found in accepting with grace that we live with limits but also in keeping an eye on the possibilities without being heroic, grandiose or naive.

The theological obstacle of a sacred-secular distinction, the failure to distinguish between vocation and career, the three classic temptations, a misguided sense of duty, and the failure to appreciate the significance of limits—this list of potential obstacles to vocational discernment is not exhaustive. In fact, possibly the greatest threat to our vocation is fear, the subject of the next chapter. Still, it is helpful to review the list and to honestly consider what is, for us, the most significant obstacle to our own vocational identity and fulfillment. Ask yourself, What is it that might undercut my capacity to embrace my calling? The more honest we are, the greater the likelihood that we will be able to confront these obstacles and, over time, "fan into flame the gift of God" (2 Tim 1:6 NIV).

Two Essential Capabilities

Our ability to break through an impasse in our vocational development comes in learning to *think* vocationally. Thinking vocationally involves two distinctive capabilities, two capacities that by themselves are of little value, but that, together enable us to think and act in truth. The first is the capacity of *retrospection*, and the second is the capacity to be *fully present*.

Retrospection. Retrospection is one of the most significant capacities of people who think vocationally, people who gracefully accept not only their limits but also their potential. It is the ability to see and appreciate our own stories and the footprints of the Spirit through the course of our lives.

Self-knowledge comes through looking back at the work of God in our lives, at our actions and at our responses to events and opportunities, at the "accidents" of our history, and to wonder how they have led to this point in our life story. If we know ourselves it is because we know our history—our personal history.

Retrospection includes, for example, appreciating the nature and character of our family of origin. What did it mean to grow up in this particular family at this particular time? How did the character and behavior patterns of our parents shape us? What is the meaning of our birth order? How did the dynamics of family life make us who we are?

But this is only one element we consider. Through retrospection we interpret how our identity and our call have unfolded in the whole of our life experience thus far. The factors that shape our sense of vocation are the elements of our identity that only make sense to us when we consider our own story, the events and circumstances of our life. Often it is in the telling of our story that we come to clarity about what is important to us and about what, more than anything else, we know we are called to do.

Sometimes through retrospection we come to the recognition that what we are already doing is what we are called to do. As we work at our task or in our role we see a reflection of something fundamental about our identity and our calling. I became the academic dean of a seminary in Manila, Philippines for no more noble a reason than that there was no one else available to fill the post! But then it became clear to me that this was probably what I was called to do. Many similar stories can be told. Some writers discover that they are called to write when they have the opportunity to write and take advantage of it, then find one writing opportunity leading to another. This is why I urge young adults to give themselves in generous service, service that may include a variety of activities and responsibilities. We discover our selves in action, and action becomes the fodder for reflection.

Retrospection also includes coming to terms with the difficult moments in our journey. We must make sense of the setbacks and suffering that shape our lives. To see how past difficulties inform our present we must reflect critically and discern how those difficult events in our lives have made us who we are. What does it mean when we have been released from a job or have been turned down for an employment opportunity? How has a closed door led to opportunities we might not have had otherwise? How has a death or a major loss in the past shaped us, informed our actions and influenced our responses? We learn who we are by reflecting on the past, by knowing and interpreting the story of our life.

Fully present. Recognizing the importance of retrospection does not mean that we should take a sentimental view of the past. There is nothing gained by nostalgic sentimentalism or by living in the past, regretfully wishing that things had been different. We must look back, but we look back so that we can be fully present to the current situation, to the current moment, to the real circumstances of our current life situation.

Everything in our lives is prelude to the present moment, to the present event, to the opportunities that are before us *now*. We are called to be fully present to this moment, to turn from regrets or nostalgia, to turn from anger at those who may have limited us in the past. We must ask how we can be fully present to a current set of needs and potential acts of generous service, now, in this moment and at this time.

What enables us to be fully present is the capacity to see our present in light of our past, in light of our story, in light of the set of circumstances and events, including our actions and reactions, that have brought us to this day. Retrospection is the capacity to think about the past in a manner that enables us to be fully present now.

A simple rule of thumb: God only leads us one step at a time. We should never overstate how significant one step or phase in God's providential guidance might be. I left seminary in the late 1970s convinced that my calling was fundamentally that of preaching. Eventually I found that while my sense of vocation *includes* preaching, that is only one part of who I am called to be. In retrospect, however, it is clear to me that preaching was a very good place for me to begin my public ministry. I am very glad that wise counsel freed me from remaining locked in one role when God was leading me to build on it and to go in another direction.

Again, I must stress that the purpose of retrospection is to enable us to be fully present. This is ably illustrated by one of my favorite athletes, the Spanish tennis professional Arantxa Sanchez Vicario. Only five feet, six inches tall, Vicario does not immediately impress one as a formidable athlete. Nobody would think of her as one of the stronger women on the professional tennis tour. What makes her remarkable is her capacity to focus.

After Vicario won the semifinal game that placed her in the 1995 Wimbledon championship match, a *London Times* journalist commented on her extraordinary performance. She was not dispirited by a bad sequence of points, she was not vulnerable to gamesmanship or to contrived interruptions by her opponent, and she refused to let poor calls by the umpires throw her off her game. Most of all, she kept her short legs going tirelessly. And she did all this in the face of the apparent athletic superiority of her opponent.

Vicario is a testimony to all of us. Many gifted people fail to achieve their potential simply because they are too easily distracted. They are not focused. Many people complain about the past or are nostalgic about it. They are bitter because something was "taken" from them or because they feel someone has done something to hurt or limit them. Or they are nostalgic about a previous chapter of their life that is now gone, for whatever reason.

Other people, in their giftedness, are "ladder climbers." They are never fully present to a situation because their focus is only on where they hope to be. Each occasion, opportunity and personal encounter is merely a means to an end.

It is true that the present chapter is but one of many in our lives, and that in the future God may lead us elsewhere. But it is vocationally perverse to work only to be noticed or merely to acquire the experience necessary to get the job we *really* want. When we approach our work in this way, the people with whom we work naturally feel used.

A pastor might recognize that he is not called to the pastorate and that he needs to explore his options and see what God is really calling him to do. But in the meantime he has a parish with real people who have real problems. He should be fully present to them while he awaits the time when God will call him to close the door on this chapter of his life.

A young college professor might acknowledge that she will not be at that particular college for the rest of her life. But in the meantime she should be fully present to her colleagues, to her students and to the mission of the college.

A stay-at-home mother knows that she will not always have children at home and that another chapter in her life will come when her focus will be elsewhere. But for now she is a full-time mother, and her children and family are the focus of her attention. She can focus on them without regret, without a longing to be freed from the burden of caring for them, but fully present, knowing that the children will grow up soon—indeed, it will surprise her how quickly it will happen.

But we are only fully present to this moment, to this time in our life, if we live and work *in light of* our past. Sanchez Vicario was never so present to the action of the game that she forgot the score. She was not ahistorical. She knew the score, and this heightened her capacity to be present to the moment. In other words, people of retrospection—people who are informed by their stories—have a greater capacity to be fully present to the events, circumstances and opportunities of the moment. Thinking vocationally is being both fully present to the moment and retrospective. The one enables the other.

Intentionality and Mindfulness

To think and act vocationally we must think and act *intentionally*. We are not merely acted upon; we do not merely react to our circumstances and to what is forced on us. Rather we respond thoughtfully, and our actions are focused and purposeful. We refuse to be victimized by our circumstances or by other people. We have resolved that our actions will not be determined by our fears or by the unreasonable expectations of others. Rather our actions will be influenced by who we are and who we have been called to be.

The bottom line is simple: Will we choose to act *intentionally*? Will we merely be acted upon, or will we take responsibility for our life, for our future? Will we live in disappointment and bitterness because we were not treated as we think we deserve to be treated, or will we let the past go—forgiving and, without recrimination, embracing the possibilities in our today and our tomorrow?

Will we resolve to act intentionally rather than automatically? Will our actions and our responses be measured, thoughtful and focused?

If we are going to live with sanity and grace in the midst of hectic noise and competing demands and expectations, we have to learn to say no. Many of us fear saying no because we do not know if we will be shutting down the very thing we are called to be and do.

We can only learn to turn aside from invitations, demands and expectations when we have clarity in the core of our being about what we *are* called to do, about that to which we must say yes. Our no frees us to say yes.

Part Two

TO BE ALL
THAT YOU ARE
CALLED TO BE

Six

COURAGE &
CHARACTER

God has not given us a spirit of fear,
but of power and of love and of a sound mind.
2 TIMOTHY 1:7 NRSV

I mplicit in these words from the apostle is the central defining
principle of this whole discussion of vocation: If we embrace our
vocation and thrive within that to which God has called us, it will
first and foremost be because we are women and men of *courage*. This is
the heart of the matter. God has not given us a spirit of fear—sometimes
translated "timidity" or "cowardice"—but a heart that the Spirit of God has
filled with courage. And it takes courage to make a difference.

It took courage for Clarence Jordan, in the late 1950s, to set up the Koi-
nonia Farm, a community of racial reconciliation in southwest Georgia. It
took courage for him to persevere in the face of the threats of the Ku Klux
Klan, to persist even when one of the facilities at the farm was torched and
the grounds strafed by machine-gun fire.

It took courage for Wolfgang Amadeus Mozart, a child prodigy who was
a brilliant pianist and could have been very wealthy with the fees from his

performances, to choose to put his energies into composition, which he had come to believe was his true calling. And we are the beneficiaries today.

It took courage for Dorothy Day, an unwed mother, social activist and journalist, to lead a movement to take in the poor and the hungry of New York City. It took courage for her to use her writing skills to call all of Christendom, but particularly American Catholics, to live with more compassion. To do so she had to confront the religious authorities of her day, with whom she was never popular.

It took courage for Reynolds Price, an American writer and novelist, not only to accept at age fifty-one that he had cancer of the spine but to confront and defy his sickness. Despite profound humiliation and horrible pain he refused to feel sorry for himself, but chose rather, in the healing that did come, to accept his new limitations. He works now from a wheelchair and has published thirteen books—novels, plays, memoirs, and collections of poems and essays—since the time when the cancer was discovered and he learned that his situation was hopeless.

It took courage for Albert Benjamin Simpson, a senior Presbyterian minister and pastor of a prominent congregation in New York City, to step aside when his congregation refused to accept Italian immigrants and to start something new, a movement that would emphasize both evangelism and social concern, that would affirm a doctrine of sanctification that incorporates both soul and body. Eventually he began the first Bible institute and missionary training center in North America, in Nyack, New York.

It took courage for Nelson Mandela to refuse to be victimized by his oppressors, to refuse to take a course of revenge against the white authorities of South Africa. As an advocate for civil rights for all residents of his country, he was imprisoned for over twenty years, often in solitary confinement. Yet his generous spirit was never broken; neither was his resolve that he would seek to overcome racial oppression. And it took courage. In 1995, a year after he became president, South Africa was hosting the World Cup of rugby. His fellow black Africans refused to support their own local, all-white South African team. In response to this crisis, he donned the team uniform; he put it on! He wore it to the stadium, and dramatically the whole country, it seemed with one voice, cheered for this all-white team. It was a powerful symbolic action, but more to the point—it was an act of courage.

"Ninoy" Aquino was first jailed and later exiled from the Philippines because he was a political threat to dictator Ferdinand Marcos. But after several years in the United States he resolved that he could no longer stay away. It took courage for Ninoy to board a plane in Boston in 1983, probably assuming that Marcos would once more put him in jail, and knowing that his life was threatened. He had, after all, made the point in a public speech in 1980 that the Philippine people were "worth dying for." Tragically, he was assassinated on the tarmac of the international airport in Manila, the airport that now bears his name. His courage inspired his wife, Cory, and thousands of others to take to the streets in February 1986, standing in front of tanks and armored vehicles and refusing to move until Marcos and his wife, Imelda, fled the country.

To celebrate courage does not mean we praise any act of bravado regardless of motives or outcomes. Many foolish things have been done in the name of courage, conviction and principle. There were white civic leaders in the American south in the 1960s who refused—courageously you might say—to allow African-American students into certain public schools and universities. This was bigotry, not courage. There are religious zealots who insist that they see the truth and who demand that others agree with them. They do so in a manner that only *seems* courageous, for true courage is also generous.

The ironic thing is that it is not courage that marks these people; it is fear. They are driven by fear of losing control, fear of people who are different, fear that their position or security or comforts or influence will be lost.

True courage has several noteworthy qualifiers: wisdom, moral integrity, gratitude, humility and patience.

Courage and Wisdom

First, true courage will always be qualified by wisdom. Sometimes we are profoundly impressed when people have grandiose schemes, visions of some remarkable future. We think they must be courageous people indeed to have such extraordinary vision. Leadership does take vision, but sometimes we lose our capacity to distinguish between a grandiose scheme and a courageous vision. With all such aspirations, we need to ask: Is this truly a courageous vision or is it nothing but hubris and presumption?

When we are tempted to be miracle workers who can turn stone to bread or heroes who can leap from the height of the temple, it helps to remind ourselves that our Lord rejected this path and chose the way of the cross. You might say that the prominent people in missionary service, the arts and government whom I identified earlier in this chapter had grand visions. That is true. But what marked them as women and men of courage was not that they had grand schemes; rather it was their determination to do what needed to be done and to say what needed to be said in the routine of every day.

True courage always involves risk—risk that your reputation will be injured, that not everyone will praise you, that you will lose influence, your home (Mandela), even your life (Aquino). But you take the risk because you choose to live by conscience. True courage might actually mean that we back away from something with a resolve to quietly leave and move elsewhere.

Wisdom and courage are partners. If an action is cavalier or irresponsible, it is not courageous. True courage is marked by prudence.

Moral Integrity

Another qualifier of true courage is moral integrity. When the apostle Paul calls us to think of ourselves with sober judgment, he also urges us not to be "conformed to this world" (Rom 12:2-3). Our point of departure should be one of moral integrity and commitment. This includes financial honesty and sexual integrity—faithfulness to one's spouse or celibacy for those who are single. Moral integrity also involves consistency of speech—being careful about what we say and how we say it and refusing to participate in lies or flattery.

Our private lives and our work in the world are part of a whole. If we have clarity of thought and heart when it comes to our sense of call or vocation, it will be because we have purity of heart. Vocational integrity—living in a way that is consistent with who we are—is only possible when we have a commitment to moral integrity.

Gratitude and Humility

True courage is also characterized by gratitude and humility. Without these virtues moral integrity is nothing more than moralism and judgmentalism. When we read that the apostle Paul advises Timothy that "God has not given us a spirit of fear, but of power and of love and of a sound mind" (2 Tim 1:7), we are reminded of a crucial and vital qualifier: true courage is always matched by humility, grace, forgiveness and compassion. Genuine courage is always complemented by a teachable spirit.

Gratitude and humility are two cardinal virtues of the spiritual life—the two from which faith, hope and love spring, the two virtues or graces that make courage life-giving.

Gratitude, or thanksgiving, is the celebration of the goodness of God, the act of living with a fundamental conviction that God is good. It represents a fundamental posture of life: to see the good, the noble and the excellent and to receive it all as sheer gift. The alternative posture is complaint—of constantly assuming that you deserve better, that you are getting the raw deal in life. While our complaint is always with others, this posture is rooted in the assumption that God is not really good.

Humility is the soulmate of gratitude, and both are the heart expressions of people who have experienced the mercy of God. Humility is the acceptance of who we are—the grace to embrace our own identity and calling rather than to live by pretense. And this, of course, means that we refuse to envy others. Humility frees us to celebrate the gifts and abilities of others rather than to feel diminished by them. Further, humility is often evident in a sense of humor, which is a sign that we are not taking ourselves too seriously.

Patience

Genuine courage is also qualified by patience. When it comes to vocation one of the great temptations is to think that what we are called to do must have particular expression immediately. The sooner something happens the better; we feel rushed and pressured, intent on accomplishing "great" things quickly.

But God works slowly; his ways are often subtle and almost imperceptible. He is never in a hurry. The shepherd David was anointed to be king of Israel. He had God's blessing and he knew the position was his; there was clarity about his call. Remarkably, however, many years passed before he actually sat on the throne. He had to wait for God's timing. In his waiting he refused to take things into his own hands or to try to force the hand of God. He refused to kill the incumbent king, his archrival and enemy, when he could easily have done so. He chose to wait for God to do his work in his time.

Then there is Nelson Mandela, who became president of the nation of South Africa in 1994. If there was ever a person who was destined to be the leader of his people, it was he. Yet he spent most of his adult life in prison, waiting. He did not fulfill his call in terms of the role of president and leader of his people until he was past what we normally think of as retirement age.

True courage is characterized by patience—patience with God, whose work is often imperceptible and slow, patience and generosity of spirit with others, and patience with ourselves.

When we are patient, we recognize that our vocation will be fulfilled eventually; we do not need to grasp after it or grab opportunities prematurely. We can eagerly engage in a study program in the present, knowing that opportunities will open up in the future. We do not need to cut short an education program just because an opportunity has opened (unless it is clear that patience has been exercised in choosing to pursue the opportunity).

If we are the parents of small children we can wait, knowing that opportunities will come in the future but that for now our priority is these children given to us by God. With patience we can accept that our options are necessarily limited during this time. We do not need to face these limitations with resentment, which the children themselves would feel; rather we should embrace the limitations with grace and patience.

Having patience does not mean doing nothing; rather we trust our future to God and take full advantage of the present, enjoying and learning from the moment and serving in the opportunities that *are* given to us, instead of sitting around waiting.

Nelson Mandela, for example, established an extensive system of study in the prison system, preparing himself and others for the day when they would provide leadership for their country.

Parents can be fully present to their children, but also see the child-rearing years as a season for reflection and study as well as a time in which substantial friendships can be formed. A person who feels called to be a professor can eagerly engage the opportunities for service that *are* given while awaiting an opening for which to apply. Patience means that we wait with grace without bemoaning lost time, without assuming that time is being wasted.

Courage must be characterized by wisdom, moral integrity, gratitude and humility, and patience. But the bottom line is still *courage.*

The Courage to Be

Genuine courage is what Paul Tillich calls "the courage to be." Although Tillich speaks as a theistic existentialist, the principle has validity even for those who do not accept his philosophical presupposition. Do we have the courage to be—the courage to be who we are and do what we are called to do?

Tillich makes the case that true courage is essentially the courage to be *oneself.* "Courage," he writes, "is the affirmation of one's essential nature."[1] This is something we often fear; Tillich notes that fear is not only the fear of *dying* but also the fear of *living.* His question really is, then: Do you have to the courage to live? When we have the courage to live, we find joy, for "Joy is the emotional expression of the courageous Yes to one's own true being."[2] This affirmation of our essential nature is rooted in a basic assumption: that our essential nature is good, something we can and must affirm and accept. God created us good. And while our essential nature is certainly distorted and confused because of sin, the effects of sin are not so great that we are incapable of coming to terms with who God has made us to be. Our redemption includes accepting ourselves as God's creation and embracing the grace that enables us to live in a way that is consistent with this creation.

In his extraordinary biography of Samuel Johnson, Jackson Bate celebrates the courage of this English man of letters. He observes that honesty was central to Johnson's courage.

> We have a hero who starts out with everything against him, including painful liabilities of personal temperament—a turbulent imagination, acute anxiety, aggressive pride, extreme impatience, radical self-division and self-conflict.

He is compelled to wage long and desperate struggles, at two crucial times in his life, against what he feared was the onset of insanity. Yet step by step, often in the hardest possible way, he wins through to the triumph of honesty to experience that [which] all of us prize in our hearts. . . .

One of the first effects he has on us is that we find ourselves catching, by contagion, something of his courage. . . .

His honesty to human experience cuts through the "cant," the loose talk and pretense, which all of us get seduced into needlessly complicating life for both ourselves and other people.[3]

Johnson was a man of profound moral sincerity. He detested false piety. He refused to be a victim and to blame his circumstances and his limitations on anyone. For him, envy was a waste of energy. But most of all, what made him a man of courage was his honesty with himself about himself. Bate calls it his "massive honesty."

Honesty About Our Fears
Courage begins with honesty about our fears. Wise people know that fears haunt us from within and cripple us if we do not face them with honesty— "massive honesty."

When government officials operate out of fear, they shut down the opposition or run from criticism and accountability to the people. When religious leaders live in fear, they "lord it over those in [their] charge" rather than leading by example (1 Pet 5:3), however legitimate or noble they make their fear appear. When parents are afraid, they become controllers and manipulators.

We rationalize and say that we do what we do in order to keep peace, or because we do not want to hurt the feelings of others, or because we are concerned for the well-being of our family, or because of some other high and noble justification. Our reasons may sound like legitimate concerns, but if we are honest they are often nothing more than rationalizations. We are really motivated by fear.

We don't speak the truth to the boss, we don't say what we know we need to say, because we fear the implications for our future job prospects. We don't speak the truth in love to friends because we fear that they will strike back at us in anger or that they will reject us.

We don't venture into a new opportunity because we fear failure and would rather continue in mediocrity than truly strive for excellence. We allow people to call us to submission when they really mean compliance, when they persuade us of the lie that compliance is the same as spiritual submission. We don't do our best at something because we fear success and the responsibility that it brings.

Acknowledging our fears does not in itself somehow make us courageous or justify our actions. But it is a start. When we acknowledge our fears, we can ask if they are legitimate; we can ask if we are really living in faith, hope and love, or whether our fears are nothing but rationalizations for actions that are less than noble. We can at least begin to move toward "massive honesty," toward an honesty about our fears that enables us to cast our cares upon our Father in heaven and become truly courageous people.

Only with courage will we have the capacity to move beyond convention, compliance and imitation and truly be who we are called to be. It takes courage to face pressure from family. It takes courage to choose our vocation in light of our own expectations when our cultural context encourages us to seek comfort, fame and power. Our fallen hearts have a natural propensity toward that which is comfortable, easy and secure. But often if we are to fulfill our vocation, we will have to act counter to these superficial propensities. The unchecked longing for wealth, comfort and security will inevitably threaten our capacity to know and respond fully to our vocation.

It takes courage to pursue our vocation, the courage to be—the courage to be true to who we are, even if it means living on the edge, living with risk, living with less security and less influence and less power—because to pursue our vocation means that we have chosen the way that is true to who we are, true to ourselves, true to our call.

When we make the transition to our senior years, it will take courage to let go of our role, our occupation and the outward forms of influence and power. Many of us will feel that we have been pushed aside and are no longer valued. The great danger at this transition is that to sustain a sense of our personal dignity and worth we will cling to titles, roles and our "influence" for fear that if we let go we will lose everything that has mattered to us. This is particularly a danger for people whose personal identity has been wrapped up in their work or in the company or organization into which they have poured their life.

When we feel the loss of influence and significance, it takes courage to let go and accept that our role will be very different. But only in letting go, the critical act of courage, do we become a source of blessing and wisdom. When we fearfully cling to our influence, we lose it; when we have the courage to let our influence go, we gain it.

We are able to live with this degree of courage, reflected in focus and passion, only if we are clear about who we are and what we have been called to do. As Parker Palmer notes, this is possible only if we live connected, rather than disconnected, lives.[4] If we feel disconnected from the work that we do, from the organization we work for, from our coworkers and from the people we serve, the resolution must come through a renewed connection with ourselves. Only as we live with this connectedness are we at peace with ourselves. Our words and our deeds have integrity because they are consistent with the fundamental character of who we are. We are not living by pretense; we are not living a lie.

This means especially that we must come to terms with our fear. We can only live connected lives, lives of focus and courage, lives of intentionality and purpose, if with massive honesty we must come to some level of resolution of the fears that so easily hound us, sap our energy and threaten our capacity to be all that we are called to be.

As Palmer notes, when we blame others, responding as victims rather than taking responsibility for our lives, we invariably do so because we have failed to be honest about our fears and about what is really driving us to a particular pattern of behavior.

The bottom line is simple: if we are not to be consumed and co-opted by our fears, we must be able to confront them honestly and somehow tame them. I suspect that in this life our fears will never go away completely, but in God's grace they can be kept at bay. Yet this can happen only if we are honest about them, if we find friends and supporters whose encouragement enables us to rise above our fears. Only then do we live connected lives— lives that find integration from the very core of our beings.

The Grace of God and the Encouragement of Others
In a fascinating study of mysticism and vocation, Canadian philosopher

James R. Horne makes the observation that mystics—people who have had a profoundly emotional experience of an external, transcendent authority—make good vocational choices because they possess two characteristics. On the one hand, mystics are certain of themselves; on the other, they are prepared to make decisions that they know involve risk.[5]

In other words, vocational integrity is a matter of both courage and calling, of having the courage to accept the risk that inevitably comes with embracing our vocation. This courage is rooted in the confidence that we know ourselves and that we have no desire to be anyone other than who God has made us to be. While self-knowledge is never absolute, we are able to know ourselves such that we can act with courage and integrity.

On the other hand, if we are honest with ourselves and with what is in our hearts, we admit that we know and feel that this world is too much for us. We are in over our heads. We live and work—at home, at our job, in our studies, in the church—in contexts and settings that insidiously eat away at our capacity to be people of courage. Our only hope is to appreciate that we are not in this alone.

Our confidence is that God goes with us and fills us with his Spirit. When the apostle Paul speaks of the extraordinary peace of God that guards our hearts and minds (Phil 4:7), he speaks of an inner serenity and connectedness that frees us to live and work and speak with courage. Our only hope for acting with courage is to acknowledge our fears before God and to receive his consolation.

We are also called to encourage one another. Paul says that he does not lose heart, meaning that he remains *encouraged*. In virtually the same breath he says, "God, who consoles the downcast, consoled us by the arrival of Titus" (2 Cor 7:6). Paul, an apostle, speaks of the encouragement that comes through a man much younger than himself.

There is perhaps no more powerful ministry that we can have to one another than the ministry of encouragement. With it we grant to one another that quality, that virtue, that intangible inner strength that enables us to rise above the fears that so easily cripple us. When we offer encouragement we enable one another to have the courage that is needed for this day, for this hour, for this moment. With encouragement we can do what we are called to do, we can follow our conscience, we can say yes to the

Scriptures when the apostle says that we have not been given a spirit of fear.

We do not walk this road alone; we are consoled by the grace of God and we walk with one another.

There are at least five points of leverage that help us to be all that we are called to be as stewards of the gifts, opportunities and potential that we have. The first has been the subject of this chapter: character, particularly *courage*. Each of the others is the subject of one of the four chapters that follow:

☐ continuous learning

☐ our capacity to live and work through difficulty and disappointment with emotional resilience

☐ the organizations of which we are a part

☐ the routine and rhythm of our lives, particularly the interplay between solitude and community

Seven

THE CAPACITY
TO LEARN

*O*ur potential for vocational growth and long-term vocational vitality exists in direct proportion to our capacity to learn. As noted earlier, change is a fundamental feature of the world in which we work. Knowing how to learn is critical to our capacity to respond and adapt to change. Learning enables us to embrace change effectively.

It is increasingly the case that we cannot assume that we will have one occupation for the whole of our life or career. Futurologists were only recently saying that the average person in the West will experience five significant occupational or career changes in the course of a normal career or lifespan of work. Now those same writers are observing that the trend has continued and that now the average number of career changes is *seven*. The obvious conclusion is that only those who are learners—continuous learners—will be able to survive and thrive.

Continuous Learners
When we ask what will enable us to "fan into flame the gift of God" (2 Tim

1:6 NIV), there is no doubt that a critical means by which this happens is through intentional, mindful, continuous learning. As Peter Senge insists, people who have "personal mastery" are those who "live in a continual learning mode," which he speaks of as a lifelong discipline. "People with a high level of personal mastery are acutely aware of their ignorance, their incompetence, their growth areas."[1] Mary Catherine Bateson aptly puts it this way: "Learning is the new continuity for individuals, innovation the new continuity for business."[2]

We must view the process of learning as something pertinent to the *whole* of who we are, not just the work that we do or that we have been trained to do. Formal academic study is just one part—perhaps only a small part—of all that it means to be a learner.

In their study *Lifelines,* Sharan B. Merriam and M. Carolyn Clark effectively show that life is fundamentally about two things: our work and our relationships. We become mature as we develop the capacity to work effectively and to live in relationship—to know how to love and receive love. We grow into our identity through our work and our relationships,[3] and Merriam and Clark contend that maturity arises in the actual interrelationship between work and love. The key to this interplay is the capacity to learn.[4] Failure in one of these two areas—work or relationships—invariably affects the other. Though work and love are distinct from one another, they cannot be polarized or compartmentalized. And this is no different for the Christian believer who rightly views both work and relationships as arising from our identity in Christ.

Both our work and our relationships offer opportunities for growth and personal development. Work is task-oriented, with a focus on achievement. Relationships are people-oriented, with a focus on feelings. The challenge of true personal maturity is to develop the capacity to be complete and effective in both areas. Merriam and Clark contend that "learning is the linchpin in this process."[5] Our lives are structured around work and relationships, and learning is the means by which we develop our capacity to work well and to live in loving relationships.[6]

We learn from family, from work and from friends. We learn from failure as well as success; we learn from being let down but also by being affirmed and loved. We learn from the complexity of daily life—from the dilemmas we face, from the problems we encounter, from the situations that inevitably cross our paths. If we learn well, we grow in our capacity to work and to love, to achieve something but also to live in healthy relationships. The goal is to be effective at what we are called to do—to become a master of our craft, you might say—but also to be people of highly fruitful and meaningful relationships, in marriage, in our family, with our friends and in our community.

Maturity is found not only in mastering each of these aspects individually but also in the capacity to resolve the demands of both, to be effective in both work and relationships simultaneously. I am an academic administrator and the father of two sons. These represent distinct areas of my life, but I am not the one without the other. I am an academic administrator as one who is a father. My effectiveness as a father is profoundly significant to my capabilities as a dean. And my responsibilities as a dean play a profound part in my contributing to the formation of my sons. My work is not isolated from my life as a member of a family.

I grew up as the child of missionaries to Ecuador. One of the perpetual debates among mission societies in the 1960s was whether it was good and appropriate for children to be sent away to boarding schools. The justification for sending children to boarding schools was twofold: that children need an American-style education and that their parents need to be free to give themselves full time to their missionary responsibilities.

Both parts of the rationale are flawed, but it is the second part that intrigues me more and more. I was away at a boarding school for my initial grade school years, but later my parents made the courageous decision—for which I am profoundly grateful to them—to confront mission authorities. They resolved that they would keep my sister and me at home and that we would attend a local school, even if this meant that they would have to resign from the mission organization. One of the many reasons for this decision was my mother's conviction that she was both a mother and a missionary and that her effectiveness as a missionary was directly linked to the fact that she was a mother.

My mother insists that she is not about to judge people who choose otherwise; many people for whom she has very high regard sent their children away to boarding schools. But for her it made no sense to have a ministry to women—young women with young children—while she sent her children miles away. She did not consider her children to be an obstacle to her ministry as a missionary. To the contrary, she ministered as a whole person, as one who was a mother. She taught women who had children as a mother who had children herself. Her mothering gave integrity, character and depth to her teaching ministry.

It makes sense, then, that as a fundamental orientation of our lives we would nurture a love of learning in both our work and our relationships. Learning empowers us; it frees us to serve more effectively. It enables us to respond to problems and challenges with minds and hearts that are capable of improvisation. If we are learners we are less intimidated by changes in the home, in the workplace and in our social environment. And if we are confident that we know *how* to learn, then we are more likely to have the necessary courage to tackle things we have never done before. When we are learners, we grow in our capacity to live in authentic relationships with our family and friends, with fellow members of our church and with our coworkers.

Peter Drucker suggests that we should always sustain two different streams of learning and self-improvement. And though he is speaking specifically about work and career, what he says is equally applicable to relationships. Drucker advises readers first to "do better what you already do reasonably well" and second to learn a new skill in response to change, in response to new opportunity and responsibility.[7]

We should continue to improve, through learning, in areas in which we are already effective. If you are a teacher, even a very good teacher, continue to grow in your capacity to teach. Learn a new approach to teaching, or adapt your teaching to new or different situations. We should also develop new skills in response to new circumstances or opportunities in our lives. We might learn a language, learn how to be a parent or learn a new computer program. As we learn these new skills we mature in true expression and fulfillment of our vocation and our relationships.

How We Learn

Learning happens in different ways for different people. Some people thrive in classrooms; some don't. Some people love to read and find it easy to learn from books. Others never learn something by reading a manual; they learn by observation. And still others learn best in the context of relationships and conversation.

Consequently, it is helpful both to identify the *different* ways in which people learn and to affirm that we each have our *preferred* way of learning. But we also need to emphasize that some things are best learned—or even *only* learned—in particular ways. So we need to be attentive to each model or style of learning. Having said this, it is wise to recognize that we have preferred ways of learning, and this is something we can exploit to our benefit.

Four approaches to learning. Though there are complex and sophisticated analyses of the different styles of learning, for a simple overview it is helpful to think in terms of *four* approaches to learning.

Some people learn best *cognitively*—through lectures and reading. The emphasis is on intellectual understanding as the key to learning, and it is assumed that learners will apply and live out the principles and implications about which they have learned.

Some people learn best *socially*—through small-group discussions where conversation is the key to learning. The actual learning comes *with* others. Wisdom, insight, perspectives and the learning experience itself are shared so that learning happens together.

Some people learn best *by doing* that which is being learned. Often this happens when a person works with a supervisor. Regardless of whether there is supervision or not, people who learn best by doing develop a capacity to learn by trial and error, from seeing and sensing what works and what does not work from the actual experience of doing something.

Finally, some people learn best *through observation.* The most comfortable way to approach a concept or skill for them is to stand outside the event, to watch from a safe distance before actively engaging the issue at hand or the skill being taught.

Consider all four approaches in more detail. Some people love books and libraries and classrooms and lectures. They thrive on the formal structures and patterns of an academic life that is structured around this approach to learning. Some people struggle with this approach not because they are not smart or intellectually capable but because this is not their preferred mode of learning.

While not everyone will gravitate to this mode of learning, it is a mode that we all need to incorporate into our learning patterns because there are some things that can only be learned in this way. Reading and listening to lectures, for example, is the best way to assimilate certain kinds of knowledge and information, to appropriate wisdom from a teacher or author. If I want to know what theologian Karl Barth taught and thought, I need to read his books. I need to find a quiet space for reflective or thoughtful reading. I need to take notes and consider what he says in light of what others say who speak to the same issues. Attentive listening and thoughtful reading are essential means by which we appropriate much that is critical to a full practice and program of learning.

But others gravitate to conversation. For them learning happens not so much through listening to a wise and competent teacher or through reading a book, but through reflective conversation, which they usually find to be most fruitful with peers—others who are at similar stages in the learning process. Social learners love to learn *with* others. These are people who discover truth through the interaction they have with others who may see things differently or who may have a different experience of the things being learned about. We learn about the way the world works by conversing with people—family, peers, coworkers and other. We learn by conversation.

When I use small groups in my teaching, I consistently notice that some students immediately gravitate to a group. They have been listening to a lecture, and now they are eager to talk—not to dominate, but to share their perspectives in a safe environment where they can thrive on the give and take of conversation. Others, in contrast, wish that the lecture would go on. You sense that they wonder why they should have to talk with others when they have enrolled in the course and have paid for it so they could hear the teacher. They roll their eyes as they wonder what value there is in talking with others who are their peers and thus know no more about the subject matter than they do.

But one of the vital means by which we learn is through conversation. Most critical, possibly, is the capacity to listen and to appreciate that others see things differently. Furthermore, it is through listening and conversation that we sharpen one another and clarify our thinking, and then begin to live in light of what we have learned. The first approach to learning—the more cerebral model—is usually highly individual; and it is often easy for a person to learn something but not live it. The social approach to learning is communal and thus can include an element of accountability. Members of the group can challenge one another: Do you live in the light of what you have learned and discovered; do you live by the principles you have discovered with us, in our group?

Some of the best learning is done by teams. People who work together need to learn together. Rather than each of us reading something and then applying it to the workplace, we can read and discuss and debate and learn together. When we learn together, through conversation, we are more likely to be able to work together effectively. Conversation, then, is a critical means by which we learn.

Nevertheless, there are some things that cannot be learned either through books and lectures or through conversation. These are the things that are only learned by *doing* them. Learning by doing is the preferred way of learning for some people, but we all need to appreciate this approach because many important things can be learned only in this way.

For example, you cannot learn to drive a car by hearing a lecture or discussing it with peers. There is no other way to learn how to drive than by *driving*. If you are using a vehicle with a manual transmission, this principle is even more apparent. No amount of previous discussion or wonderful lectures will give you the feel for that clutch. You can only learn how to release the clutch by feel—by doing it yourself.

The same applies to prayer. We can only learn to pray by praying. Again, while there is certainly a place for lectures on prayer and group discussions on prayer, if we are going to learn contemplative prayer—the practice of being in and responding to the presence of Christ—we will learn it by doing it. For both learning to drive and learning to pray there is great value in having a teacher or a mentor. But rather than lecturing, the mentor will come alongside to help explain what is happening and why. In both cases we learn by trial and error, from fleeting moments of success that incrementally lead us to some level of mastery. This is also the way we learn to play a musical instrument or master an athletic skill.

Finally, some people find that the most fruitful way of learning is through *observation*. People who prefer to learn this way have high powers for seeing what is happening and for imitating it. They prefer to learn by watching what someone else does and then doing it themselves. When shown how to do it, they can do it.

Again, while this is the preferred way of learning for some, learning can be enhanced for all of us if we can develop the skill of learning by observation. Much of what I have learned about teaching has come from watching master teachers—not just from listening to their lectures, but also from observing how they manage the class and how they respond to students. Athletes know that they have much to learn by watching the premier athletes in their sport. But they will learn by watching only if they develop powers of observation—being attentive and noticing what is new, what is different and what is significant.

Observation is also a critical means by which we learn about people, especially about people who are different from us. This is why the experience of travel can be so informative. It enables us to see and to appreciate differences—the diversity of humanity and of human experience. Travelers are not the same as tourists. To travel is to be with and among a people. Tourists, whether by choice or not, inevitably become the center of attention. Travelers, on the other hand, intentionally stay to one side and do not draw attention to themselves. And because of this, travelers make better learners than tourists.

We learn about the organization in which we work by observation, by watching and sensing what makes the institution unique and what defines its culture and ethos and way of doing things.

Of these four different ways of learning, consider two things: First, recognize your preferred way of learning and exploit it. Build on it, celebrate it and enjoy learning in your preferred style without apology. If you love libraries, then enjoy them. If you enjoy learning through conversation, then don't let others minimize your capacity to learn because you are not as drawn to quiet libraries as they are.

How one approaches learning is an integral part of self-knowledge. Be observant of how you learn, of how you have approached new situations in the past and of how you have learned new skills or responded to new opportunities. How have you adapted to changes both when your adaptation has been effective and when it has not? In particular ask yourself which approach to learning you enjoy and what learning situations have brought you the greatest joy. The approach to learning that you most enjoy is probably the most fruitful mode of learning for you. Identify honestly the situations in which you struggle to learn, in which learning is a chore for you. You need not avoid the approach to learning that is a struggle for you, but it does help to recognize that learning in that mode will not come easily to you.

Second, we also need to master the capacity to learn through *each* approach. There are some things that are learned only or can be learned best through one of these specific approaches to learning. If we are going to grow in wisdom and maturity and in our capacity to thrive in our vocation, we will need to learn through each approach.

Learning requires patience. Learning always takes time. True learning is the fruit of patience. There is no quick way to learn how to play the flute; it is learned by *doing*, and practice and years of patience are required before it is mastered. This also applies to each way of learning. People who are masters of child psychology have spent countless hours watching children. There is no way to master their field quickly. People who have the capacity to discover a new asteroid are people who have mastered the ability to observe the heavens; because of their patience they know when something in the sky is new or different.

Each approach to learning requires time and patience; there is no such thing as instant education or learning.

Evaluation and review. Furthermore, each way of learning is strengthened when we allow ourselves to be reviewed and evaluated, when we welcome and learn effectively from critical assessments of our work, our accomplishments and our efforts. Many of us, unfortunately, feel threatened by evaluations. We fear the judgment of others and feel diminished by any critique that calls for change or that points out an area that merits improvement. But if we are going to master anything, literally anything, we need to learn through the observations and critiques of others.

We can learn from people who have already mastered our craft, as an aspiring flutist learns from a master flute player. We can learn from peers who observe and comment on our work. And we can learn from people we serve, people who comment on the way we teach or provide a service. Good companies regularly solicit comments from their customers so that they can serve them better.

There is little value in flattery. The book of Proverbs contains warnings about people whose words do nothing more than inflate our egos. Flattery is actually equated with lying. We all need affirmation, but we do not need empty praise. We can only learn and grow if we are not crushed by criticism and if our heads are not inflated by praise. We must take criticism and praise in stride and learn from both.

Further, in reflecting on these approaches to learning, we can ask ourselves the questions, Where and how should I give myself to the task of learning? Which approach will be the most beneficial at this point in my vocational journey? Some people, regardless of age, need a formal education, a program of study in an academic environment that leads to an academic degree. But not all people, even young people, need a formal program of study. We should not so idolize formal education that we minimize the value of other forms of learning and their significance in a person's long-term vocational development.

There are many people who come to clarity about their vocation in midlife and recognize that to thrive in their calling they will need to go back to school or pursue some other form of study. If we pursue a program of study, we should pursue it because we want to learn. Many people go back to school in midlife not only to get a degree but to prove to the system that they already know all they need to know—they only need the "paper to confirm it." This attitude wastes everyone's time, especially the student's. If we go back to school, we go to learn.

Another question can be asked: What would strengthen my capacity to thrive vocationally? Perhaps you have a Ph.D. in physics, but you know that as yet you do not teach effectively. The challenge then may be to find out how to teach by reading, by taking a seminar or by having someone visit your class and critique your teaching. For some of these resources you may have to look outside the physics department where you are so comfortable. But resolve to learn how to teach well!

Mentors. We need to affirm the significance and potential of good mentors in our lives. When I recognized that I did not know how to pray and resolved that I must learn, I sought out Dr. Alex Aronis, a pastor in the city where we lived, and asked him to teach me. He taught me a great deal but eventually suggested that I approach another person, Father Thomas H. Green, S.J. The knowledge that I have about how to pray has come largely through the generosity of these two men. They gave many hours of their time to talk with me about my own prayers—not about prayer itself or the phenomena of prayer, but about *my* prayer and how it was progressing. They were mentors and coaches. They were on the sidelines while I did the learning, but I could not have learned without them.

I learned as much about how to pastor a church from monthly afternoon meetings with a senior pastor, Ronald Unruh, in the city where I first pastored, as I did from any other source, including books. What a gift he gave me! An afternoon once a month for conversation, during which he encouraged me and responded to my questions.

My seminary education was not unimportant; rather there were some things that could not be learned except in the actual context of ministry. It has become commonplace in recent years to berate theological schools for all that they are *not* doing. Some people have even published books with lists of all they did not learn in seminary, a parallel to those publications that list everything someone else did not learn in business school. But such a posture is simplistic. There are some things you can learn only in seminary and some things you can learn only while actually in ministry. I learned much more about preaching while I was in a regular routine of preaching than I could possibly have learned in seminary. Still, what I learned in seminary about preaching was essential and critical to my capacity to learn how to preach while I was preaching. We need both the capacity to learn in the context of formal education and the capacity to learn while on the job.

What we learn while on the job will often come through another person, a teacher, a guide, a counselor or a spiritual director. These mentors are gifts. Most of all, they bring hope. The genius of good mentoring is the capacity to bring hope and encouragement, believing in people so that they can learn, grow and embrace all that they are called to be. The genius of learning from a mentor is found in a posture of eager attentiveness that reflects a longing for wisdom and a longing for learning. But because some of us are so confident in our own wisdom or are incapable of saying that we do not know all we need to know, we never know the joy of being mentored.

Learning and Wisdom

We learn skills. We learn how to be effective in relationships. We learn history and theory. It is easy to summarize all the different things that we might learn and the different ways in which we learn. But we need to find a center—something that integrates our learning, giving focus to it and ultimately enabling us to mature as individuals through it.

Wisdom gives us this center and brings focus and integration to our learning. Surely our deepest longing is to be women and men who in wisdom, knowledge and learning can bring depth of character, understanding and skill to our work and our relationships. Perhaps nothing matters vocationally as much as becoming wise. In the book of the Proverbs we find these words:

> Get wisdom; get insight: do not forget, nor turn away
>   from the words of my mouth.
> Do not forsake her, and she will keep you;
>   love her, and she will guard you.
> The beginning of wisdom is this: Get wisdom,
>   and whatever else you get, get insight. (Prov 4:5-7)

In the end, no one will care how successful you were, or how much you accomplished, or how important you were or what roles you had. All that will matter, the older we get, is whether we are wise women and men.

The pursuit of wisdom provides focus and integration to our learning, for the wise person is mature in relationships as well as work. Wisdom also provides depth, the conviction that what we long for is not merely knowledge or information but learning that enables us to mature as persons. Wisdom is not the comprehension of abstract principles or profound truths so much as it is the capacity to respond to the developments around us with strength, to have the skills to embrace change and new challenges with ingenuity and to become mature emotionally through difficult setbacks and disappointments.

For the LORD gives wisdom;
    from his mouth come knowledge and understanding;
he stores up sound wisdom for the upright;
    he is a shield to those who walk blamelessly,
guarding the paths of justice
    and preserving the way of his faithful ones.
Then you will understand righteousness and justice
    and equity, every good path;
for wisdom will come into your heart,
    and knowledge will be pleasant to your soul;
prudence will watch over you;
    and understanding will guard you. (Prov 2:6-11)

Wisdom enables us to live and work, to sustain our relationships and our work in our lives with integrity, focus and balance. It includes the grace of accepting that we are growing older and embracing the implications of the transitions of our lives, such as the possibilities and the limitations that will come with our senior years.

In our pursuit of wisdom, we attend to history and stories, for the wise see the present in light of the past. In the pursuit of wisdom we seek deep understanding so that we will be people in whom there is both depth of conviction and a focus that is not self-centered or superficial. The pursuit of wisdom is eminently practical, for a wise person longs to make a difference. The pursuit of wisdom keeps us from learning theories that have no practical application. Finally, the pursuit of wisdom integrates mind and heart. A wise person is interested in knowledge that informs the whole person and enables us to live in truth. Wisdom is not just cerebral or analytical; it includes our emotions and our bodies. To grow in wisdom demands that we learn to think and act holistically.

Wisdom, Learning and Experience

One of the key means by which we grow in wisdom is the discovery, understanding and application of truth or knowledge. Another key means of growth in wisdom and thus growth in learning is *retrospection*, one way in which we think vocationally. Retrospection is a critical means by which we *learn*. Wise people know that in both work and relationships, growth and development result when we have the capacity to make life itself the curriculum from which we learn, when we recognize the power of lived experience and have the ability to reflect on our own story as well as those of others. C. S. Lewis puts it this way:

> What I like about experience is that it is such an honest thing. You may take any number of wrong turnings; but keep your eyes open and you will not be allowed to go very far before the warning signs appear. You may have deceived yourself, but experience is not trying to deceive you. The universe rings true wherever you fairly test it.[8]

Learning from experience requires that we develop two skills: observation—to see what is going on around us and in us, and improvisation—to take what we have learned from experience and adapt it to a new life situation. And all the while we are learning. Learning is continuous; it is threaded throughout the whole of our lives. New circumstances regularly and consistently require that we adapt, experiment, adjust and change. Education is less and less a matter of *preparing* for life and work, and more and more a matter of life and work *itself*. To live is to learn—to grow in wisdom as we draw from experience and make sense of and respond to new circumstances. The only way we can adapt to new circumstances and do better what we already do well is to learn from past experience.

The bottom line is this: we must never grow complacent. We must never grow tired of learning. For as soon as we stop learning we lose the capacity to grow and mature in our work and in our relationships. Continual learning enables us to grow in wisdom; through learning we experience personal transformation. Through learning we acquire skills, and through learning we discover ourselves and our potential, developing a more expansive and holistic life perspective. And we can learn from everything, everyday, from observing the pattern of life and human responses in a doctor's waiting room, to listening to people around us on the bus as we travel to work, to reading the morning newspaper.

Learning from our experiences does not mean that we draw simplistic insights or become reductionistic, deducing a moral from every last thing that we come across. Sometimes a certain experience or observation only begins to make sense years later, when we draw on other experiences and a range of observations to respond with courage and wisdom to a new situation. Learning from experience means being *attentive* to life and people and circumstances, and most of all to ourselves and to our own responses and reactions along the way.

Whenever we learn, we are expanding our heart and mind; through learning we become people with depth and breadth of soul. For example, when I began to learn how to pray, although it was only one skill, it was part of a new way of understanding God's work in my life. When people learn a language, they enter into another world; a new language gives them another way of seeing life and people and relationships. And we cannot begin to calculate the value of the gift that is given to children or adults when they learn how to read.

Mary Catherine Bateson puts it well:

> Learning is perhaps the only pleasure that might replace increasing consumption as our chosen mode of enriching experience. Someday, the joy of recognizing a pattern in a leaf or the geological strata in a cliff face might replace the satisfactions of new carpeting or more horsepower in an engine, and the chance to learn in the workplace might seem more valuable than increased purchasing power or a move up the organizational chart. Increasing knowledge of the ethology of wolves might someday replace the power savored in destroying them.[9]

But this will only come about, as Bateson implies, when we come to see knowledge as a source of delight rather than as a means of power. We enjoy learning because we enjoy discovery, the expansion of heart and mind, and growth in wisdom, not merely because it is a means by which we can accomplish something. And if we are learners, we can take on any challenge, any change in our circumstances or environment, without fear.

Through learning we experience personal growth and transformation. Hence my suggestion that our potential for vocational growth and development is in direct proportion to our capacity to learn.

Eight

THE CROSS
WE BEAR

Difficulty &
Emotional Maturity

*I*t is a simple fact of life: there will be difficulties, setbacks and disappointments. For some people there will be rejection; for others
there will be tragic losses. For still others there will be inexplicable
suffering. No one is immune from pain; it is part of the package that comes
with life. This is a broken and cruel world. God is good, but life is unfair.
God is good, but the fact remains that whether we fulfill our vocation outside the church or inside it, neither the world nor the church is fair. All people will experience the brokenness of the world intersecting with their lives
in a thousand and one ways.

Two things, then, must be stressed. First, we should not be surprised by
difficulty. We should not be derailed or overly perplexed when it comes.
When people respond with great surprise to the difficulties that hit them, I
wonder if their mother ever told them that life is not fair. Difficulty surprises many of us in the "First World" because our lives are so comfortable;
we are lulled into assuming that things should and will always be this way.
But our ease is illusionary; we must remember that most of the world lives
with difficulty and suffering that is daily and chronic.

Second, it is clear that we need to make sense of difficulty and to see what significance it has for our capacity to fulfill a vocation. As we shall see, there is hardly anything more critical to personal and vocational development than the nature of our response to difficulty, setbacks, rejection, disappointment or suffering. The evidence that we have responded effectively is that we develop emotional maturity and resilience.

Making Sense of Pain

We need a sustaining theology of pain and suffering. Without one, we will never be able to live with sanity in the midst of the setbacks and disappointments that we will inevitably experience. We need a theology of suffering that is both biblical and congruent with our experience. In this regard, I find three texts of Holy Scripture to be particularly helpful.

First, in Romans 8, beginning with verse 17, the apostle Paul makes an extraordinary statement and assumption: that when our identity is in Christ we will experience difficulty, setbacks and disappointment. Such experiences are inherent in what it means to be a Christian. If we are heirs with Christ we will suffer with him. It is as simple as that. We cannot conclude from Holy Scripture that if we are Christians we will have an easier road than will people who are not Christians.

But although Christians suffer, and thus experience the same pain that others encounter, there is a difference: we suffer with hope. This is the way in which being a Christian makes a fundamental difference. Our faith gives us a different perspective from which to live through those times when pain intersects with our lives.

In Romans 8 Paul uses the image of the woman in childbirth. He makes the observation that the whole of creation is groaning as though in labor, reminding us that our own pain is but part of the pain of a broken and fallen world. But the image of labor and childbirth also gives us perspective on suffering. Imagine a woman in the pain of childbirth who has no idea what is happening to her body! In contrast, the pain is no less for the woman who understands, but she experiences it as one who longs to see and hold her newborn child. In the same way, we need not despair when pain and difficulty intersect with our lives; we experience suffering as those who see the big picture, as those who know that in the end all will be made well.

Second, in 2 Corinthians 4—6, the apostle draws another conclusion: that our capacity to be life and grace to others comes through our very experience of difficulty. We are "clay jars." As such,

We are afflicted in every way, but not crushed; perplexed, but not driven to despair; persecuted, but not forsaken; struck down, but not destroyed; always carrying in the body the death of Jesus, so that the life of Jesus may also be made visible in our bodies. For while we live, we are always being given up to death for Jesus' sake, so that the life of Jesus may be made visible in our mortal flesh. So death is at work in us, but life in you. (2 Cor 4:8-12)

Our ability to make a difference for God in a broken world, both outside of the church and within it, comes through our capacity to be life in the midst of death, to be people of hope in a place of discouragement.

When Paul speaks of his own weakness, indeed boasts in it and in the glory of God evident in it, he is not speaking of toleration of mediocrity. Rather, Paul makes clear in 2 Corinthians 12 that his "weakness" is the difficulty—the obstacles and setbacks—that is inevitably a part of his ministry. And clearly it is his conviction that this difficulty is the vehicle by which God brings life and grace to others.

Third, in Romans 5 we are reminded of the simple principle that suffering, setbacks and disappointment are the very means by which we are formed into people of maturity and strength. We might wish it otherwise. There is no doubt that suffering has broken many people and left them disenchanted, bitter and lifeless. But the fact remains that it is through the stress points of life that our character is tested and proven. As the apostle puts it: "suffering produces endurance, and endurance produces character, and character produces hope" (Rom 5:3-4).

But everything depends on our response. Suffering and pain either break us or make us. Through it all we either become angry, bitter and cynical or, with grace, grow through endurance, become people of character and signals of hope in a dark and dispirited world.

The real test of vocational and emotional maturity lies in our capacity to handle difficult and painful times. It is through these stressful events—whether in relationships or in our work—that we mature in faith and grow in self-knowledge. It is through difficult and painful times that we come to greater and greater clarity about what really matters to us and about what priorities must guide our life choices, in the end learning to love and to be loved even in the midst of difficulty.

The choice is always ours. As a Canadian who has spent half of his life overseas—first as the child of missionary parents and then as a seminary professor, dean and later pastor in the Phillipines—I am struck by a characteristic of my culture and society: the inclination to feel *victimized*.

John Ralston Saul identifies "victimization" as a kind of *Canadian* sin or propensity. He uses the example of the regional political movements and describes how they are nourished on the idea that one region of the country is the victim of another region or of the federal government. He notes that it is little wonder that these movements have little vision for the whole country. Then he writes powerfully about the dangers and foolishness of this posture: "All of us, it can't be denied, are victimized from time to time. But this is quite different from believing ourselves to be victims all the time."[1]

There is a great tongue-in-cheek line attributed to Robert Orben that captures this feeling of victimization: "Sometimes I get the feeling that the whole world is against me, but deep down I know that's not true. Some of the smaller countries are neutral."

We are "victimized" when we get lost in a sea of self-pity, live with a martyr complex and carry our hurt around like a chip on our shoulder, becoming more and more cynical, having lost the capacity to live with grace, humor, compassion and patience. Victimization robs us of life.

Viktor Frankl's work has helped many to see that suffering is the real test of whether we transcend self-absorption and truly "live for others." Suffering imparted meaning and purpose to Frankl's life,[2] and through his experience he came to see that the genesis of our values is to be found in our suffering. That is, life has meaning and values; but this meaning and these values are discovered, owned and sustained by the ways in which we confront and respond to the evil around us and to the suffering that it entails.

It is critical that we learn to respond positively to difficulty, setbacks and disappointment. In its essence the issue is one of perspective, of living with and accepting the simple reality that God is good but life is not fair. The genius of our response ultimately rests on whether we will allow ourselves to be victimized, or whether our very difficulty and suffering will become a means of grace to ourselves and to others.

Social critic Stephanie Golden makes the astute observation that many self-help recovery groups encourage the victims of abuse to focus so much of their attention on the abuse and on the abuser that their primary sense of identity becomes the fact that they are victims. Tragically, this very posture can disable them from ever getting past the abuse. Golden draws on the insights of others who note that when this happens, victims of abuse ironically see themselves as special because of the abuse. The powerful image of the victim can blind them to their own imperfections and failings. Golden notes that:

> This grandiosity, compounded by self-righteousness and fueled by anger, often characterizes people who present themselves as victims. It is easy to fall into it, for when you feel powerless, the virtue accorded the victim seems the only route to some form of respect and to a feeling of entitlement. . . . The sense of being righteous and special is part of what makes the role of the victim so attractive.[3]

So attractive, she suggests, that some actually go so far as to create a kind of bogus victimhood that, ironically, "provides a reliable, ongoing sense of virtue."[4]

This is not to minimize for a moment the reality that many have experienced deep wounds and irretrievable loss. It is merely to say that we cannot remain perpetually victims. And the crucial question is how we respond. Are we consumed by ourselves and filled with self-pity and anger, or does our very encounter with pain become a vehicle by which we are a means of grace to others? The issue is not whether we experience difficulty; that will inevitably happen. We will not be treated as we should be treated. We will not be thanked as much as we should be thanked. We will not be affirmed or appreciated as much as we deserve. Less competent people will get positions for which we were more qualified. We will be overlooked and not appreciated because of false perceptions. We will be misunderstood, underappreciated and wrongly accused. The issue is how we respond.

The great danger is not only that we will respond with self-pity or, worse, a martyr complex. These responses are doubtlessly pathetic, but the great danger is bitterness and cynicism. It is far better to go into life and ministry with the assumption that no one owes you anything (and that God will affirm and bless you in his time). Only then can you begin to respond positively to setbacks, difficulty and disappointment.

Responding Positively

What does it take to respond with grace to difficulty and pain?

Forgiveness and the resolution of the past. First, we can only respond positively to current developments if we have already come to terms with our past and have come to resolution of the ways in which pain has intersected with our lives. For this, we must practice forgiveness.

We begin by forgiving our parents. This is fundamental. We have not all been grievously wronged. However, no parent has been perfect; no parent has been all that we wish a parent would be. Consequently, we must forgive and in compassion let go of any resentment we might have against our father or mother.

For some people this will mean coming to terms with deep wrongs. Some people have been abandoned and have never met their mother or father; worse yet, some people have been physically or emotionally abused. Some parents in ignorance have not given the child all that might have been given. They did their best, but as every parent knows, our best is never good enough. My wife and I can easily look back and see how we might have done things differently. But there is no changing that; there is no going back to assure that every hurt and pain is removed from the consciousness of our two sons.

We will remain forever locked in resentment if we do not begin with something so fundamental as forgiveness for our parents. Forgiving them is one of the most important lessons and actions of our lives. And while we need to forgive what was wrong, in our parents and in our childhood, we need even more to appreciate and affirm what is *good*, what is of God, in our parents and in their generation.

The resolution of our childhood experiences involves more than just forgiving our parents; it also includes reconciliation with all that our parents represent—the spiritual, cultural and social heritage that shaped us as children. For many it will extend into a religious or denominational heritage. In many cases it is easy to look back and resent, deeply, the wrongheadedness or the narrowness of a fundamentalist perspective. But while we must move on and embrace a broader notion of truth and life, we can never sever our roots. We have to come to terms with them.

Some people are lost nostalgically in the past. Others are eager to cast the past off as so much garbage. But to do so is to discard both the good and the bad. The truth is that we are only able to make a lasting contribution, regardless of our vocation, when we celebrate and embrace the good, and gently, though firmly, discard what is less than good. This demands a gracious discernment that includes a fundamental gratitude for all that was and is good. Only with this discernment can we build on what is positive in our heritage.

This forgiveness must be extended to others as well. One of the givens of life is that we will be wronged. We will be wronged by family, by coworkers, by the boss at the company where we work. It is not merely that we will not be treated as we deserve to be treated; we will also be *wronged*. Some people will take advantage of us. Others will speak ill of us and through gossip or slander seek to destroy our credibility. There is a multitude of ways in which we can be wronged. But the point remains: our only hope for vocational vitality over the long haul is to learn to let go of resentment.

If we are wronged while working for one organization and we carry that resentment on to the next place of work or ministry, we will infuse our work with resentment and it will destroy our capacity to live and work well. We may cover it up for a while and with a pleasant temperament and quiet resolve seek to be gentle and to carry on. But if we carry unresolved resentment in our heart it will come out in ways that deeply undermine our capacity to thrive. The most telling signal is that we will express our anger in inappropriate ways. One of the sure signs of unresolved resentment is anger that is disproportionate to the wrong. When a colleague "blows up" over something that, while wrong, simply does not deserve that response, I can only assume that there is something from the past that is still lurking in the dark shadows of his mind and heart.

Resolution of the past also must include self-forgiveness. It is so easy to look back with regrets and to wish we had done things differently. We may regret that we cut short a program of study or we may regret that we are living now with the consequences of a profoundly foolish pattern of behavior. Or perhaps we regret simply that we were not all that we could have been—to our children, to our friends, to our deceased parents, or to our coworkers in the organizations where we didn't work as effectively as we could have.

Forgiving ourselves is, of course, possible only as we come to accept God's forgiveness. I have found that my own experience of forgiveness has been most significant when I have been able to confess sins to a trusted spiritual advisor or director, and have heard the other declare aloud, "In Christ you are forgiven; go in peace." I cannot help but wonder if something was lost when Protestants moved away from oral confessions in which the personal, one-to-one assurance of pardon was given and received.

The bottom line is that we seek and hopefully find the capacity to forgive ourselves. Nothing is gained by living with regret. Nothing. Forgive yourself; learn from what has happened and what you have done. And move on, embracing the new moment and the new opportunity. Regret can so easily become nothing but self-pity, another form of self-centeredness and self-indulgence. This may be an agonizing and difficult process, but we must persevere until we have some freedom from the past.

Seeing and accepting our limitations and losses. To respond positively to the pain of life we need not only to forgive but to come to terms with losses and limitations. With each of the major transitions in our lives—from adolescence into adulthood, from early to mid-adulthood and from middle age into our senior years—we make the transition well when we recognize our limitations. Each transition includes seeing, accepting and then actually embracing our limitations. And each transition makes us conscious of those limitations in a different way. Parker Palmer reminds us that

> Each of us is given a nature by God. To have a nature is to have both limits and potentials. We can learn as much about our God-given nature by running into our limits as by experiencing our potentials. . . .
> The truth is that I cannot be anything I want to be or do anything I want to do. The truth is that my created nature, my God-given nature, makes me like

an organism in an ecosystem: I thrive in some roles and relationships within that system, but in others I wither and die.[5]

But often our encounter with these limits is painful. We are rejected when we apply for a job, or we are fired because we simply lack the necessary abilities or potential for a job or a position for which we longed. Sometimes the pain we experience results from the dashing of expectations and hopes. We had longed for a position that we have come to realize is beyond or perhaps not aligned with our abilities.

If we are honest we usually realize that our dashed expectations were often rooted in a desire to impress others. We had dreams and aspirations that were unrealistic. It is not so much that we have failed as it is that we have not achieved what was really unachievable. We have been confronted with our limits.

For some people this happens early in life; for many, if not most, of us it comes closer to mid-life when it dawns on us that we are not going to achieve all we had hoped to. We will not be a millionaire, or we will never get a Ph.D., or we will never have children, and nothing in medical science is going to change that. Whatever the hope or aspiration, it is dashed, and we are confronted with limits.

Other people are faced with physical limitations, recognizing that they do not have what it takes to be a professional athlete or that because of a serious accident they will spend the rest of their life in a wheelchair.

Whatever the limitations we face, we will not live with joy unless we learn to accept our losses with grace and choose to live in peace within the limits of our lives. As Palmer writes, "The truth is that every time a door closes behind us, the rest of the world opens up in front of us. All we need to do is stop pounding on the door that is closed, turn around, and see the largeness of life that now lies open to our soul."[6]

The way to experience joy and vocational vitality is to accept what is— regardless of the pain that it may represent for us—and to embrace the opportunities that *are* before us rather than to bemoan what might have been. When we do embrace our true opportunities, "the world opens up in front of us," in ways that can be simply uncanny. This only makes sense if we live with the assumption of God's providential care. God is over all and cares for all. And though we can accept that God allows evil, our funda-mental theological posture must be one of living in the confidence of his love, provision and direction. Moreover, our confidence also rests in the assurance that God's grace is greater than sin and that he is always working by his gracious power to bring good from evil. It is essential to remember that while God's timeline is never the same as ours, he works to bring about his purposes. Our confidence in his providential care frees us to trust God to do in his time what only he can do.

I am regularly reminded of the story of Nelson Mandela, who spent over twenty years in prison as a political prisoner, much of it in solitary confine-ment. He could easily have come out of the experience bitter, angry and dispirited; instead he came out with more life in his eyes than was there when he went in. He quite simply chose to accept what was rather than to beat his head against the limitations that were forced on him. He chose to live with hope that one day change would come and that in the meantime he would make the best of the situation in which he found himself.

Accepting the pain that is inherent in our vocation. First, we come to resolution about the past. Second, we accept graciously the limitations of our lives and circumstances, including the losses that this may represent. But we need to go further.

If we are going to thrive in our vocation, we also need to accept that some form of difficulty or pain is actually *inherent* in what we are called to do. Jesus began his public ministry with a clear sense of call (Mk 1), and he was able to say at the conclusion of his ministry that he had finished the work given him by the Father (Jn 17). But he could not finish that work unless he accepted the cross—the way of Calvary. Furthermore, Jesus advises his disciples that we are to take up our cross and follow him. When we follow Jesus, we follow him to the cross; we bear a cross. Consequently, it is reasonable to conclude that in some form a cross will mark *every* voca-tion; there will be some way in which the pain of a broken world intersects with our call.

In some cases we need to graciously accept the fact that difficulty is part of what it takes to achieve a particular end. The cost of being a first class athlete or musician is rigorous training, practice and work. Many talented individuals who are very good musicians or athletes never become accom-

plished for the simple reason that they are not prepared to pay the price—
the hours and hours of training, rehearsal and practice, far away from any
kind of affirmation or praise. In this sense, the pain or cross may be the
effort that it takes to accomplish one's ends.

In other cases, the cross may be something that attends the role or
responsibility itself. For example, you cannot work effectively in administration if you need to be affirmed and recognized every time you do something helpful. It is inherent to the job, much like in the role of parenting or
homemaking, that a great deal of the work that a person does goes unno-
ticed and unappreciated. If you cannot accept this with grace then you are
better off staying out of administration.

As an artist, you will never find the support and affirmation you need in
a culture that is fundamentally pragmatic. As a businessperson, you will
always live with the ups and downs of the market and of consumer trends.

As a teacher, you will consistently be amazed that people who seemed
to understand what you taught never really got the point, or if they did
understand, did not appreciate everything and do not live in a way that is
consistent with what they have learned. Jesus faced this also, as when
Philip said to him, "Lord, show us the Father, and we will be satisfied" (Jn
14:8). Our students' lack of understanding or appreciation is never an
excuse for poor teaching; rather we should recognize the inherent burden or
difficulty that attends good teaching.

As a surgeon, you will save many lives, but you will also lose some—
including some that you know could have been saved. As a politician, you
will never be able to satisfy all of your constituents, and many who support
you at one point can so quickly turn against you.

In other cases the reality of the cross may come not so much through
that which attends a task, as through the unique circumstances in which we
are seeking to fulfill a particular calling at a particular time. The cross may
be that while you know your calling, you have limited options to do what
you feel called to do because you need a waged job to sustain your livelihood. Or it could be that you have a dual identity, as both an administrator
and a writer, or as both a teacher and a mother, and it seems that the two
sides of your life and work are always in tension and competition with one
another. In fact the two sides are probably in some significant way essential

for one another. Whatever the case, difficulty is inherent in some way in every line of work and at the heart of every vocation.

The point at which difficulty intersects with our lives and our work is not incidental; it is central and significant for at least two reasons. First, it is here that we encounter our own need for God and grow in dependence upon God. It is, then, a means of grace to us. Where we feel the mark of the cross in our vocation is the locus wherein we grow in dependence on God for his all-sufficient grace. The author of the book of Hebrews speaks of the cross as something that Jesus endured "for the sake of the joy that was set before him" (Heb 12:2). It was a necessary means for the fulfillment of his vocation and of his joy. The cross, then, marks each vocation not as a limitation but as the very means by which God enables us to know joy through the calling and work that he gives us. We must learn to accept graciously the way that this pain intersects with our lives, our work and our vocation.

Second, the point at which the cross intersects with our lives is also the very place where we are grace and life to others. At the point of our weakness, at the point where we feel "death . . . at work in us," we are life to others (2 Cor 4:12).

But the place where the cross intersects with our lives will only be a means of grace to ourselves and others if we reject any propensity toward self-pity because others do not see, feel or appreciate our difficulty. The cross becomes a means of grace when it is accepted with patience, grace and submission, with the quietness of a meek heart. Herein is not weakness, but strength; and herein we are women and men who truly live and bring life to others.

Incidentally, many people fall into the trap of attributing their difficulties to the evil one—to some form of demonic opposition or attack. Sometimes when I read missionary newsletters or hear people in business report on their work, it seems they believe that every difficulty they experience is due to the direct work of the evil one and his demonic host. While in principle this is certainly possible, most of the difficulties we experience are simply part of what it means to live on planet earth or are inherent in our vocation and thus clearly allowed by God. To attribute all difficulty to the evil one is to give evil more credit than is due. In so doing we easily fail to embrace difficulty as a cross through which God is bringing grace to bear in our lives and in the lives of others.

Responding positively to failure and setbacks. Finally, we will suffer with grace only when we learn how to handle failure and setbacks. Responding positively, with emotional resilience, to setbacks, failure and rejection is one of the most crucial capacities of vocational development and expression.

It is very easy for us to feel profoundly sorry for ourselves when we struggle with substantial health or family problems. But few things cut off joy and vocational vitality quite like self-pity. Invariably, people who thrive in life and work are those who learn the power of gratitude, hope and faith in the midst of darkness and pain.

We will become angry, bitter, hard people if we do not develop the capacity to accept with grace the setbacks of life and work, setbacks resulting from our own failures or from the actions of others, justified or unjustified.

Sometimes our sense of failure is based on unrealistic expectations. We fail ourselves by failing to be all we hope to be. All that is really suffering is our wounded ego. But it still hurts!

In other cases we were living with false notions of success. Rather than being content in our work, in this place and at this time and with these people, we hope to be heroes and to solve all the problems. We struggle with accepting our limitations. We struggle in the realization that we cannot do everything, that we cannot be responsible for everything that happens in the organization and that we can only be accountable for our work and our situation.

Sometimes our potential for success is limited by the performance of others. Wisdom demands that we accept this with grace.

But in other cases, we *have* failed. As we look back we can see the failures that might have been avoided if we had exercised more foresight. In this kind of situation, humility demands that we accept that we are not that good at something or that at least on this particular occasion we did not do good work. As a preacher you did not preach a good sermon and there is no particular excuse; as an investor you made a bad investment and you or your clients lost money; as a mechanic you did not do a good job on a car repair and the customer is demanding that it be done right. There are no excuses, no extenuating circumstances and no way to avoid the simple fact that you failed.

To thrive vocationally we must accept this with grace and move on. We do not need to be defensive; we do not need to dig for excuses. We can acknowledge that we are not perfect, that we will learn from our mistakes, that even though we failed it does not mean that we tolerate mediocrity. We can press on with faith, hope and love.

It is important to acknowledge failure. Often when we are unwilling to acknowledge failure, we remain in a situation that will only get worse; all we do by staying is reinforce the failure. Further, we often are inclined to overstate the significance of failure. We tend to be crushed by it when we should probably merely close that door of our life, cut our losses and move ahead. And when we do there is often more ahead of us than we could possibly have imagined. In time, especially if we learn from our mistakes, what happened will become an increasingly distant memory.

Suffering and careerism. Thinking about difficulty is one point at which reflection on vocation parts ways with careerism. The great danger of thinking only in terms of career is not only that we might miss our vocation but that we might fail to appreciate the significance of suffering. When we think in terms of career, we can be inclined to assume that our life and our work will represent a single, rising curve as we move up the ranks. We so easily get caught thinking that we do what we are doing today only because it will position us for the next slot we hope to fill.

But the fact of the matter is that people lose farms, lose jobs and experience other major setbacks. Good pastors who will be very effective over the long haul are released by congregations. Missionaries find that all their training seems to be meaningless in the face of intense difficulty and opposition. People in business experience great losses. Gifted and capable politicians lose elections.

Thinking vocationally means accepting that difficulty is not an aberration but an inevitability in our career development; accepting difficulty as a factor of growth is an integral part of accepting our vocation.

Emotional Development and Resilience

The capacity to handle difficulty, suffering, disappointment and setbacks is an essential element of long-term vocational development. How we handle a major setback, failure or loss may be one of the most—if not the most—critical factors in our life-long vocational effectiveness. This applies equally whether the setbacks are our fault or the fault of others.

Fundamentally, emotional maturity and resilience are at stake. The issue is not so much difficulty itself as it is our capacity to be people of heart: able to respond emotionally, from the center of our beings, to the ups and downs of life, work and relationships. Only as we come to terms with our joys and sorrows can we truly be all that we are called to be. Nothing represents maturity as much as *emotional resilience*. We remain perpetually adolescent if we fail to develop emotionally. Furthermore, emotional maturity or resilience is our primary resource when it comes to vocational identity and development. Emotional resilience enables us to respond with strength to setbacks, disappointments and the changes and challenges that will inevitably come our way.

We may be inclined to say that one particular factor is the most critical in our vocational development, the most significant in our capacity to achieve our potential. Some people will say that nothing matters more than character, others will say that nothing is as critical as our capacity to learn, and still others will focus on the capacity to suffer with grace or the ability to work within and through organizations. But emotional development may be the factor that more than any other determines whether we will become all we are called to be. It is the thread that runs through each of the five points of leverage in our personal and professional development. Lack of emotional maturity and resilience will sabotage our life and our vocation. Intelligence, giftedness, hard work, dedication and opportunities will all be forfeited and wasted.

I grew up within a Christian subculture in which emotions were viewed as incidental or secondary at best. People who were emotional were in some way suspect. We tended to view cerebral or rational people as deep, profound and trustworthy. People who were deemed emotional were not to be trusted and were generally considered to be superficial. Gender stereotypes were also involved. Frequently women were portrayed as more emotional and therefore less competent, rational, dependable and trustworthy.

But the focus on emotion within Holy Scripture has helped me to learn that this cultural standard was completely backward. There is a powerful emphasis on joy in the ministry of Jesus, who says explicitly that he came so that our joy might be made complete (Jn 15:11). There is a marked emphasis on emotion in the writings of the apostle Paul, who speaks of "the peace of God, which surpasses all understanding" and which will "guard your hearts and your minds in Christ Jesus" (Phil 4:7). Emotions are probably most evident in the Psalms, the prayers of the Old Testament that arise out of the depth of human passion. They are preeminent demonstrations of emotion.

People of depth are those who have learned to live from the heart—from the core of their being. People of depth have learned the power and truth of responding emotionally to God, to his creation and to others. Perhaps there is nothing more crucial to our call to become Christian, to mature in our faith, to love God and others, than reflection on our emotions.

When people are weak and immature, it is not because they are emotional but because they *lack* the capability to express a whole range of emotions and to express them in a manner that is appropriate to the occasion. Their feelings are erratic; they express great anger over minor inconveniences, and an unreasonable fear undermines their capacity for elemental human joy and camaraderie. Only those who are emotionally mature are capable of responding to the ups and downs of life and work and the crises that inevitably come our way. In my experience it is men who, as often as not, fall short in this regard, men who come completely unglued when they are suddenly overwhelmed with a crisis or a problem. But all of us, men and women, urgently need to learn and grow together in our capacity to live emotionally, and to grow toward emotional maturity.

The signs of emotional health. What, then, are the signs of emotional health? What does the goal toward which we should reach look like, the goal of emotional maturity and resilience that enables us to grow in faith and wisdom and in our capacity to fulfill our vocation?

You are a person of emotional health if:

1. You know your feelings and are able to draw on them in making significant decisions rather than having your decisions sabotaged by your emotions. You are able to manage your emotional life so that you are neither paralyzed by depression[7] or worry nor swept away by anger. You manage your emotions; you are not managed *by* your emotions.

2. You are able to persist in the face of setbacks and disappointment and able to channel your emotional energy toward worthy goals. You are willing to live with delayed gratification.

3. You are able to recognize the feelings of others and as appropriate, empathize with them; you are able to handle the emotional aspects of relationships with grace. Your own emotional state does not undercut your capacity to listen to and identify with others. You can speak openly and frankly, with grace, patience and tact, and say what needs to be said even if it will stir up the emotions of others. You have the capacity to handle the anger of other people with grace, even when that anger is expressed toward you. You are not paralyzed by fear of other people's responses—their anger if you have a difficult thing to tell them, or their mourning if you have sad news to share. This does not mean you are uncaring. Not at all. You empathize. But you are not fearful of or sabotaged by the emotions of others.

Within an organization or group you have a sensitivity to the group process that enables you to be alert to emotional responses and to dimensions of community life.

4. You are able to express your emotions honestly in appropriate settings, whether ardent devotion or anger or disappointment, whether to God or to a spouse or friend or child or colleague. Your emotional response is appropriate; your anger, for example, corresponds to the wrong. You do not lose your emotional keel; you do not lose your temper when angry. You do not take your anger out on your spouse or child, or in your anger cast another person in the wrong light. You air your feelings of discouragement where there are confidants who can work through the disappointment with you and where your comments will not be misunderstood or misread.

5. You do not use emotional blackmail to get your way, threatening to resign if you do not get what you want, withholding favors or good will because someone is not fulfilling your expectations. You respond with openness and honesty but also with grace toward those with whom you differ, particularly family members and coworkers. Moreover, the fear of hurting your feelings does not keep others from acting according to their convictions or conscience. They are not straight jacketed by fear of your emotional reaction. They do not have to fear your anger or your loss of temper; they do not have to worry that your feelings would be hurt.

6. You are able to respond to both praise and criticism with grace: you are not crushed by criticism; your ego is not inflated by praise. You do not crave affirmation, and you are able to respond to criticism with grace rather than undue defensiveness. You do not deflect criticism; you do not blame the bearer of the criticism or someone else so that you can neither hear nor benefit from the feedback.

The final and most critical sign of emotional health is the capacity to respond with sorrow—with anger, mourning or discouragement—when pain intersects with our lives, but always to come back to an emotional center of *joy*. In the end, a person of emotional maturity is an individual in whom the dominant emotion is joy—joy rooted in confidence in the goodness of God, trust in his providential care and hope in the ultimate triumph of justice and peace.

One of the signs of emotional *immaturity* is that we are not able to distinguish between genuine difficulty and suffering and the vicissitudes of life. Bad weather is not suffering; traffic delays are not suffering. These are just part of life. On the whole, emotionally immature people are irritated or frustrated with those things that we merely need to take in stride as part of life on planet earth. They find minor inconveniences to be signs of great injustice against them. When it comes to these elements of our lives we merely need to bear with one another, bear with the weather and live in a fundamental posture of gratitude, humility and patience.

The way to emotional health. How do we get there? How do we become people of emotional maturity? Quite simply, we do so through the same "massive honesty" of which I spoke in chapter six—an honesty with what we are feeling, with what is happening inside of us and with what this means. Only with this honesty can we accept that we are emotional beings. But more, only with honesty can we live in truth and then, through that truth, come to joy.

If we are *angry,* we are angry. Anger itself is not a sin. But it is a sin if we lose our temper or if in our anger we do that which clearly violates the call to love or justice. Moreover, anger is a sin and destroys us when we carry the anger in our hearts from one day to the next. For some reason when we sleep angry, the anger scorches our souls and it becomes a bitterness from which it is very difficult to recover. My father used to say, "Keep short accounts with God." This has such an immediate application to anger. We will be wronged; nothing can stop this. But *we* can decide if those wrongs will fester in our hearts and ultimately destroy us, or if we will let them go.

We lie to ourselves when we deny that we are angry. To feel emotionally hurt or crushed while insisting that we are not angry is nothing but a denial of what is actually happening in our hearts. Emotional health comes through acknowledging our anger and then letting go. We must do both; we must acknowledge the anger, but then we must refuse to live in it.

We will become *fearful* simply because we are vulnerable. Only if we are entirely out of touch with life can we suggest that we never feel anxiety. But we walk the way of death when we allow anxiety to consume us and overpower us. Our only hope, again, is to honestly confront our worries and fears and to accept with grace that all we can do is trust in the providential care of a good and almighty God.

We will become *discouraged.* We live in a discouraging world. But if we remain locked in discouragement, we become cynical, with hearts that are in a perpetual state of gloom. There is nothing wrong with getting discouraged, but then we must receive the encouragement that comes our way. We must allow ourselves to be encouraged through the glory of a new morning or the kind words of a friend, through the testimony of Scripture or the witness of the Spirit to our hearts, through the frolicking of a dog in a park or the smile of a child. Those of us who are prone to become discouraged risk the grave danger of getting lost in self-pity and cynicism, a pit from which it is so difficult to climb.

We will all experience *loss.* Our only hope is to mourn our losses honestly. Denial defeats us. It saps energy and keeps us from moving on. With denial we become locked in the past and live falsely. I recently read that it probably takes a year to recover from a major loss—the death of a parent, for example, or the loss of a job. It takes time. For some it may take much longer than a year. And the only hope for emotional recovery and strength is to accept this, to mourn the loss and to allow God to heal our hearts in his time. In the end, if we have the capacity to be grace to others in their pain it is because we have learned to mourn our own losses and then to minister to others out of the consolation we have received from God. The apostle Paul speaks of this in 2 Corinthians:

> Blessed be the God and Father of our Lord Jesus Christ, the Father of mercies and the God of all consolation, who consoles us in all our affliction, so that we may be able to console those who are in any affliction with the consolation with which we ourselves are consoled by God. (2 Cor 1:3-4)

Many people have experienced a great loss but have been left unchanged; they have managed to shelve the experience or to push it aside so that it does not touch them. They have not been changed by it; they have not mourned. When we know people who have experienced profound loss, we are prone to say that they are doing very well if they are composed and dry eyed, carrying on with a stiff upper lip. But the danger is hypocrisy. Does our outward appearance really reflect what is happening in our hearts? Another danger is a hardened heart, a heart that has experienced loss but has not been changed.

It is far more encouraging when people who have experienced loss are actually in mourning, overwhelmed by the pain—not self-centered, but still feeling the loss deeply. Their mourning should encourage us, for then we can be fairly certain they will come to emotional strength; then we know they will have a capacity for joy.

We only know emotional maturity and resilience when we learn to open our hearts to God and to one another. There is no other way to discover and sustain emotional growth and health than with a strong *vertical* connection to God and a vital *horizontal* connection to others. The first speaks of the priority of solitude, of the individual, private encounter with God. The second speaks of community and conversation. We need both.[8]

Nine

WORKING WITH
& WITHIN
ORGANIZATIONS

W *e fulfill our vocation in partnership with others. The most* obvious form or expression of partnership is found in our relationship with the organizations in which we work and through which we invest our lives and our energies.

An organization is any formal association of individuals who are working together toward a common end, who have a mission they hope to accomplish together. This applies to congregations as well as to businesses; it includes everything from volunteer associations to educational institutions. An organization can be something as large and complex as the American government system or something as small as the association of two people who have agreed to work together on a common cause—perhaps on only a short term project, perhaps to start a business together.

The assumption that underlies organizations is simple: we are more effective working with others than functioning as hermits. It is easy to think of organizations as agencies that limit us. Our boss or the board seemingly restrains our potential or restricts us. Some of us are inclined to think of organizations as necessary evils. But organizations are the appropriate context in which to fulfill our call. When people work together, the end product is greater than the sum of the parts. Through synergism we can do greater things together than any one of us could conceivably do alone.

Organizations at their best empower us by granting us the opportunity, the encouragement, even the training to excel. Organizations at their best force us to stretch beyond our perceived limitations and enable us to discover our own potential—something we might never have seen or discovered if we were hermits. Organizations can probably best be thought of as gardens; through the discipline or husbandry of a gardener, we are able to flourish to our greatest potential. Indeed we can only hope to fulfill our vocation if we learn the grace and strength of working with others, in partnerships that enable us to be stewards of our gifts and opportunities.

I say, "organizations at their best." But even when organizations are not at their best, we still need them. No matter how gifted you are, you cannot achieve your potential in isolation from others. Wayne Gretzky is the greatest hockey player ever, a remarkably gifted athlete. But if he were to compete alone, even a group of young teenagers could probably win a game against him. For him to suggest that he is going to compete alone would be nothing short of sheer foolishness. In fact, of course, part of the genius of a player like Gretzky is his capacity to work with others; this is largely what has made him an extraordinary athlete.

The greatest musicians need coaches and mentors and composers and orchestra halls that are managed by others. A writer needs an editor and a publisher, and a publisher needs writers. No one can fulfill a vocation alone; we all need associations, partnerships and structures that enable us to work collaboratively with others.

Consequently, if we are going to be all that we are called to be, and to respond with skill, courage and grace to the call of God on our lives, we must develop the capacity to work with others in the context of organizational life. Furthermore, we need to see how our individual vocation can fit within specific organizations. We need to develop the capacity to recognize the organizations in which we are likely to be most effective.

We also need to see the dangers; organizations have particular qualities and characteristics that can actually threaten and impede our capacity to be true to who we are and who we are called to be. That is why we must exercise discernment and, of course, courage. We need to know when it is wise, vocationally speaking, for us to resign or to accept that we are leaving an organization. The goal is to discover and enter into an organizational partnership that most enables us to fulfill our vocational identity. The organization will be one that in the end does not serve us but rather provides us with an avenue by which we can be of service to Christ and others.

How We Can Be Effective Within Organizations

As we consider how we fulfill our vocation in partnership with others, we begin by examining how we can develop the capacity to be effective within the organizations in which we work or in the partnerships we form for other reasons. An example of the latter is our connection with a congregation in which we enter into the company of others to worship, fellowship and serve together. The principles or practices for effectiveness within organizations are simple; they essentially involve the capacity to live in community. We will be wise to identify and embrace the qualities that specifically enable us to work with others toward a common goal or mission within an organization. These principles are as applicable to people working in a large business as they are to two individuals who together are teaching a Sunday school class.

Character qualities. Mature character is the most critical characteristic that enables us to work effectively within organizations. If we are involved in recruitment, we must evaluate and verify that the essential quality of mature character is present in a candidate for a position. Mature character includes both the humility and courage to live by our own conscience and the ability to live and work with others with grace, patience and kindness. There are distinctive character qualities we can nurture and seek to strengthen that are directly related to our capacity to be effective in partnership with others.

First, regardless of what role we have within an organization, we are most effective when we are good *listeners.* Whether we are president or assistant manager, board member or caretaker of the plant, salesperson or donor, our capacity to be effective is directly related to our capacity to listen. Effective leaders listen to their constituents; effective donors attend to the activities and plans of the organizations to which they consider giving their dollars; effective salespeople are those who listen to what customers are saying as they shop; effective companies are attentive to their customers, seeking as much feedback as possible. They listen.

Second, effectiveness in organizations demands *dependability*. People who work with us, whether as peers, subordinates or superiors, must know that we can be counted on to do what we say we will do. We must be people of our word. We must not overpromise because of misguided generosity. At the same time, our colleagues must be able to relax when something is on our desk because it will be done when we said it would be done. We must be dependable. We must be there when we said we would be there; we must be on time with meetings, appointments and project deadlines.

Dependability is a constant, living illustration of the words of Jesus when he notes that those who are faithful in small things will be entrusted with much. Many people take lightly what appear to them to be small issues or responsibilities and then wonder why they do not get promotions or other opportunities. The reason is often simple: they were not diligent and careful in what they viewed to be secondary matters.

Quality and depth of character also involve the care we take to *respect others* and to sustain their dignity and reputation. People who thrive in organizational life work with a fundamental assumption: each person with whom they live and work is a person of worth, dignity and value. And all people are treated as such regardless of their competency or effectiveness. Even people who must be released because they did not perform their duties well or because they violated trust—perhaps by stealing organizational funds or sexually harassing a coworker—deserve to be treated with grace and dignity. Those to whom we report deserve the dignity and honor appropriate to their role or office; those who report to us are not pawns but partners without whom we would be helpless. Our colleagues deserve to know that we will not speak ill of them behind their backs or slander their character through innuendo or unfair criticism.

Nurture the three character qualities: develop your capacity to listen; be faithful and dependable in whatever is given to you, big or small; and resolve to treat everyone with whom you work with grace, dignity and honor.

Think globally; act locally. Mature character is fundamental. But our effectiveness is also reflected in the way we approach our work. People who are effective within organizations are those who have learned (to borrow a phrase from social activists) to *think* globally and *act* locally.

We are most effective, regardless of our particular role within the organization, when we do our *own* work well—when we "act locally"—in a way that takes account of the big picture. We work not in isolation but with the whole organization in mind. This principle intersects with everything we do within an organization—whether it has to do with finance and budgeting or with communication and cooperation.

The labor union leaders who have been most effective are those who have recognized that the company must make a profit and that the company must have a president and that the president must be able to lead. Only when they recognize this can the union be effective. And just as surely, managers who are effective over the long haul know full well that they are utterly dependent on a quality group of employees and colleagues, people who, in order to do their work well, need to know that their rights, benefits and working conditions are cared for.

Most literature on what makes for effective organizations is written for those in leadership or management. But all of us long to thrive within an organization in a manner that enables us to be consistent and faithful to our own identity and call. The center on a football team may never carry the ball, and he may never score a touchdown, but if his team wins it is in part because on each play he knew and executed the plan. He knows what his role is within the big picture, and he knows that without his contribution no one else will be effective.[1]

We are effective, then, when we think and act in terms of the whole—in terms of three distinct but interrelated components of organizational life: the organizational mission, the organizational budget and communication.

First, few things are so critical as thinking in terms of *mission*. What is the purpose of this organization—not just on paper but in terms of what this group of people is seeking to accomplish? How can I do what I do in a way that contributes toward that mission? What are the underlying values of the organization and how can I function in light of those values? We should know the history of the organization because that will provide primary insight into its mission, its values, its character and its potential.

Most importantly we should know the mission and work toward it. We must always remember that the mission is not *our* agenda for the organization; a mission is always made up of the common commitments of those who work together toward the common objective. The mission will evolve and develop; but it will consistently be a reflection of the organization's character, history and fundamental values. For example, you are almost certain to fail if, as a leader, you import a vision that does not fit this organization at this time. And you are almost certainly doomed to frustration if, as the organization evolves and its mission adapts to new possibilities and opportunities, you remain in the past, nostalgic for what the organization used to be. Rather we should embrace and work with others toward what God is calling this organization to do today in response to current circumstances and possibilities.

Second, we must work conscientiously in light of financial realities in the organization. We must ask ourselves: How does *money* function in this company or church or school? People who think about the big picture realize that we are colleagues and that budget issues affect everyone. One person or department cannot hope to be effective in the long run if they regularly maneuver funds for their individual agenda or department in a way that does not take account of the whole. We need to consider what is strategic and know that our own area of responsibility may not always legitimately demand new money. We can grow in our appreciation of the fact that if there are budget cuts we must work with everyone to keep the whole organization healthy.

Perhaps most of all we must learn to be stewards of the resources available to us, exploring ways in which we can creatively do more with our limited resources. Nowhere is there more danger for selfish patterns of behavior than when it comes to money; here, more than in any other area of organizational life, we need to regularly check our hearts and motives and consistently turn toward a posture of both humility and service.

Third, we are effective in fulfilling our vocation within an organization when we live and work with a commitment to *effective communication*. If we are thinking about the big picture and seeking to work together in a common mission, we need to communicate well and to pay attention to what others are seeking to pass on to us. Consider the question, and ask it regularly of yourself: How can I communicate well and be attentive to the communication of others? If we are partners we need to listen and we need to speak. We need to hear what others are saying—whether they are communicating by way of formal pronouncements or memos, or by casual conversation in the hallway.

This principle applies to what *we* are doing as well. To be effective we must communicate! We need to develop the habit of asking, Who needs to be informed of what I am doing or of what I know so that we can all be effective together? When we know something, we should consider, Who else needs to know about this, and how can I make sure they know in a timely manner? What am I doing that others need to know about—for their sake and, ultimately, for all of our sake? People in management or leadership need to appreciate that the rest of us are most effective when we are well informed. Good leadership requires effective and thorough communication—not the kind of communication with which we are only showing off what we are doing, but the kind of communication that enables all of us to see the big picture.

Usually the more people know the more effective they can be. Organizations that withhold information sometimes do so unwittingly; either the leaders are careless or they simply do not appreciate how important it is to keep their people informed. But in some cases the withholding of information is a means of keeping control (a fundamentally parental posture toward one's colleagues); it is, in a subtle way, an abuse of power.

My wife and I often worship in churches where an order of worship is not printed, and we find it perplexing. Why do these churches withhold simple information about where we are and where we are going in the worship service? Wouldn't we all worship more effectively if we did not have to wonder what is coming next? When the information is withheld, is this not a subtle form of control? This is certainly not always the case, of course; in many congregations all around the world, it has never been the practice to provide an order of worship. Nevertheless, this as an example of an area in which communication might be helpful. The main point is simply this: To work well with others we need to communicate so that others are informed.

Thinking about the big picture requires attentiveness to the *mission*, to *finances* and to *communication*. But the flip side of this equation is that while we *think* globally we must *act* locally. We must think big picture and act with a commitment to effectiveness and quality within our own sphere of responsibility. We must pour our energy into the place where we can make a difference, into our own assignment.

All people have the capacity to be effective within their own sector, department or area of responsibility. Few people are content with everything that happens in every part of the organization. But nothing is gained by complaining or fretting or belaboring the point about those things we cannot fix or those things that are really not our responsibility. Rather we must focus our energy on being able to say in the midst of the whole, "I will do what I do well. I will establish an island of excellence in the areas for which I am responsible." And that excellence will be defined in terms of the whole organization—in terms of its mission, its finances and its need for effective communication.

Think in terms of complementary capacities. We are most effective within organizations when we learn to think in terms of *complementary* competencies and capacities. We enter into the formal associations of companies and organizations because we need one another in order to achieve a common goal or purpose.

We are most effective when we see, appreciate and rely on the complementary strengths, abilities and perspectives of others. And we can do this only if we have a clear sense of who we are and the gracious humility to *accept* who we are. At the same time, though, this means that we celebrate the strengths and abilities of others. We should not feel threatened or diminished by the character strengths and abilities of others; rather we should celebrate them and depend on them, allowing their strengths to be the complement to our limitations.

Most literature that urges people to stop working so hard and to delegate more fails to address this fundamental question: Have we learned to trust and depend on others? In other words, it is not merely a matter of lightening our workload; it is also a question of the way that we think. Do we see ourselves as threatened by others or as working in tandem with others? Do we permit others to fulfill their duties, to fulfill the responsibilities that have been given to them? Do we accept the necessary role that leadership plays within the organization? To accept the role of leadership and to accept the decisions of others that affect our work requires trust in leaders or peers who are making decisions on behalf of everyone.

We will live with perpetual frustration if we seek to control everything in the workplace and fail to freely allow others to function in ways that inevitably will affect us. Board members of not-for-profit organizations should remember this too. They need to be board members, freeing those who are in leadership or staff positions to do their work, the very thing they were hired for. This too requires trust. To think in terms of complementary capacities demands that we learn to depend on one another; and this means that we must grow in our ability to trust others.

Learn how to share power. Everyone in an organization has power. Everyone. This includes the customers of a department store, whose power is most evident when they refuse to buy something. It includes the secretary who manages the flow of information to and from an office.

Traditional organizations work with the assumption that power flows in one direction—from those in power to those without power; this flow is viewed not only as unidirectional but also as coming from the top. But increasingly we are seeing that people who are effective have learned to work *collaboratively*, using the power inherent in their role or place in the organization as a means to enable others to be effective.

I am convinced that effective preaching is never merely the fruit of diligent preparation and careful delivery; good preaching happens where there is a congregation of attentive listeners who through their demeanor and the posture of their response elicit an effective ministry of the word. Boards and presidents of academic institutions are profoundly naive if they do not realize that faculty have a powerful and influential voice—as well they should. For boards, presidents and faculty to be effective together they need to share power. In each case it is a matter of affirming the character of the power that each individual or group has. As constituents we have the power to elect our national government officials, but then we must free them to do their work, with appropriate structures of accountability. As members of a congregation we have the power to elect our lay leaders, but then we need to free them, within appropriate structures of accountability, to lead the congregation.

Effective organizations thrive where there is a pattern of *shared* power. In congregations leadership can and must come both from the lay church council and from the paid pastoral staff, but each provides a different kind of leadership; power is shared, and each leads in a different way. In academic institutions all parties have a leadership role, but each role is different and complementary; faculty and administration, for example, affirm the role of one another and work together to a common end. And there is no reason why the sales personnel cannot be a major source of genuine leadership within a department store. After all, they can give management a read on what customers are saying and on how customers can be served most effectively.

We will thrive in the organizational environment only if we are not threatened by the real power of others and if we know how to work collaboratively with them regardless of where we fit in the structure of the organization. This means that we treat others first and foremost as colleagues—rather than as people who report to us or to whom we report. Furthermore, working collaboratively means being able to function even when it is not clear who has the final word and when there is no need for the buck to stop anywhere. That is, it means working effectively with others in a peer relationship, where no one involved has positional authority over another or where positional authority is not a significant point of reference as people work together.

Working collaboratively also means thriving through our capacity to listen well and to depend on complementary strengths, through our resolve to negotiate win-win outcomes for all parties. Most of all we will thrive when we come to our working relationships with a commitment to empower others, to see how we can help others to be effective in *their* work. This means, of course, that we must not use our power to undermine the effectiveness of others or to bypass their input into the process of decision-making. Whether we are acting individually or corporately we must always ask: How can we make others more effective through our actions? How can we do this in a way that enables all of us to achieve our goals?

One of the most valuable means of fostering effectiveness within organizations is to be people who can *learn* with others. Learning together may take time and patience since the habits of working and learning independently sometimes run deep. But when we learn *together,* our propensity to compete with one another or to blame one another for problems is torn down. When we learn together, we grow in our capacity to adapt to change together and to depend on one another in the midst of the changes and opportunities that are before us.

Working together includes having honest conversations about what is happening and learning to respond openly, without being defensive or protective of our personal space or of the resources we have invested in the process. Our capacity to work together as women and men, exploiting the strengths that both genders bring to our decision-making processes, is critical in this respect. Increasingly we will find that cross-gender partnerships will strengthen our workplace and the other contexts where we work with others. But these partnerships will not work if our conversation is patronizing, defensive, manipulative or filled with innuendo. We work well together when we learn to converse well together.

Everyone has power. People who thrive in an organization find ways to use their position and influence in a manner that is empowering for others. In other words, they are servants. All of this is but one dimension of what our Lord means when he says that if we are going to be "great"—individuals who fulfill powerfully who we are and who we are called to be—it will be as we learn to be servants (Mk 10:43, 44).

Accept and work within the limits and strengths of the organization. We thrive within organizations when we work with and through the actual circumstances and potential of our situation rather than constantly fighting the limits and boundaries that we invariably face. We accept the limits and build on the strengths of the organization.

This means *accepting* the limitations that are inherent in a situation; but more, it also means seeing the potential within those limits. Sometimes an organization lives with self-imposed limits that are bandied about because of fear or lack of vision. We must not overstate the limits; to do so is to inhibit the potential we have together to accomplish something significant and lasting. That being said, however, it is imperative that our vision of the possibilities be rooted in what is prudent. Wisdom, courage and true vision are not at work when someone has aspirations that are not congruent with the *actual* situation and the *actual* potential of the organization. Wisdom, courage and vision are partners; true visionaries are wise people.

This does not mean that we tolerate mediocrity; rather it means that we pursue excellence within the context of our particular situation and its potential rather than constantly complaining about what we wish *did* characterize our situation.

Two great sources of wisdom, Reinhold Neibuhr and G. K. Chesterton, provide insight in this regard. Neibuhr beckons us to accept what we cannot change, to take on with excellence what we can change and to recognize the difference between the two. This is not fatalism; it is humility. More than that, it is wisdom.

Chesterton gives us the spiritual framework from which to think through Neibuhr's model of response to our circumstances. Chesterton wrote a wonderful introduction to the Charles Dickens novel *David Copperfield* in the Everyman series. It is remarkable writing. When you begin reading Chesterton's comments, you cannot help but wonder why the publishers asked him to write the introduction because he carries on at some length— two to three pages—with his description of what he calls Dickens's "monstrous errors." You have the impression that he was not at all inclined to recommend that anyone read the book. But then he writes:

> Any fair critical account of Dickens must always make him out much smaller than he is. For any fair criticism of Dickens must take account of his monstrous errors, as I have taken account of one of the most monstrous of them during the last two or three pages. It would not be honest to conceal them. But no honest criticism, no criticism, though it spoke with the tongues of men and angels, could ever really talk about Dickens. In all of this that I have said I have not been talking about Dickens at all. . . . I have been talking about the gaps of Dickens. . . . I have been talking about the omissions of Dickens. . . . In one word, I have been talking not about Dickens, but about the absence of Dickens. But when we come to him and his work itself, what is there to be said? What is there to be said about earthquake and the dawn?[2]

What strikes me so deeply when I read the words of Chesterton is that it is easy to be a critic. It is easy to identify what is *not* present and what is *not* good and what you wish would make an organization better. But true genius has the capacity to identify the strengths and work from them, to build on them and celebrate them, being grateful for what is there rather than complaining about what is *not* there. Not that we should be passive in the face of obvious problems that need resolution; rather we should work constructively for change within the specific horizons in the organization. We should build on the strengths that are there rather than constantly complaining or berating leadership or bemoaning things that are not as we think they should be.

To function effectively within these strengths requires that we live with a fundamental posture of gratitude for these strengths. It is this posture of gratitude that empowers individuals and groups to be catalysts for positive change in the organizations in which they work—or, in the case of congregations, in the fellowships in which they worship and serve.

Learning to be effective in the midst of change. People who are effective within organizations are also those who are prepared to adapt to and be effective through change. Only people who are effective in the midst of change will have long-term vocational vitality. Change is a constant in every organization. Missionaries experience changes in the mission board; salespeople experience changes in the way business is done; educators experience changes in the way teaching happens; church members experience changes in congregational life. Change is a constant.

Effective organizations are those with a high capacity for flexibility, adaptation, innovation and change. And people who thrive *within* organizations are those with a high capacity for adapting to change. I remember once patiently listening to a board member at the college where I used to be the dean. He was complaining that things were not like they used to be there at the college, not like they were in his days as a student. While there is no doubt that some changes are less than positive, his was a sentimental nostalgia; his complaints were rooted in unreality. Organizations change. Either we accept and embrace this or we live with an unrelieved burden—a burden that is reinforced with every change.

We thrive amidst changes when we maintain a fundamental flexibility, a capacity to adapt to those changes and to see them as opportunities for growth and learning. Some changes mean that we will have to leave an organization, but most changes call us to adapt, to adjust the way that we exercise our strengths in a particular organization at a particular time, and to consider how we can thrive in our ever-changing environment.

Finding Congruence

Most fundamentally, to thrive vocationally within organizations we must find congruence between ourselves and the organizations in which we serve. In 1996 and 1997 I was involved in an extensive study of the vocational vitality of professors in Canadian seminaries. Senior faculty members in Roman Catholic, mainline Protestant and evangelical schools were interviewed. The results of our research left us with several fascinating insights. One of the most notable observations was that faculty members over the age of fifty-five who were viewed by their colleagues and students as vital and alive felt a fundamental congruence between their own values and vision and those of the school where they taught. And the majority of these faculty members had, at some point in midlife, left one place where they had taught, and where they were likely appreciated, seeking a setting where there would be a high congruence between themselves and the school.

People who have vocational vitality are in organizations whose missions they own and whose values they can identify with. Herein lies an important principle for understanding vocation: to thrive in our vocation we need to seek congruence, to find an organization with which we have a high level of identification. There is no need to hurry this if we are young. But as we come to midcareer, congruence is something we can and must think about. For many of us this should happen by our late forties, but we should remain flexible and respond to opportunities as they become available to us.

Some people will never find this congruence. Sometimes lack of congruence is due to a character problem: it represents nothing more than a lack of willingness and resolve to work with others. Some people move from one organization to another, through one crisis after another, changing jobs and hoping to find the perfect place to invest their energies, hoping to finally get the level of affirmation they think they need to be effective. But no organization is perfect; every group or company or institution has its problems. Many times when we make a move in order to get away from problems we merely exchange one set of difficulties for another.

But sometimes the lack of congruence means that we really do need to explore the possibility of making a change. For some people an inability to find congruence reflects a call to become entrepreneurial. They need to start their own business where they can have direct influence on the vision and values, or plant a new congregation rather than inherit a parish that is the fruit of another's work, or leave employment at a newspaper and become a freelance writer.

These options are not a good fit for me. I am not entrepreneurial in this sense. I am inclined to identify with organizations where I can build on what has already been accomplished or strengthen the organization as it is working through change. But other people will find vocational fulfillment and integrity only when they embark on a journey of their own.

While we are called to fulfill our vocation in partnership with others through formal associations or organizations, there is always the danger that we will align our own personal identity too closely with a particular organization.

Some of us cannot envision the possibility of working with any company, organization or church group other than the one with which we currently work. We are, in a sense, married to the company. But we will never come to full vocational integrity unless we define ourselves as *distinct* from our work, occupation and career and from the organization in which we serve. That is, we are never truly ourselves unless we maintain a fundamental distinction—or to use the language of family systems theory, a *differentiation*—from the entities or organizations in which we work.

When we fail to sustain this fundamental differentiation we almost invariably get caught up in an unhealthy dependency on the organization. Some people see an organization, whether a church, a mission or a business, as a kind of parent. They find in their workplace the love, acceptance and community that they never got from their real parents. They look to their fellow workers for the emotional support that can only come from family, friends and church. Love and unconditional acceptance are basic needs; but we cannot look for these in the organizations where we work.

Those who seek this level of affirmation and security from the organizations in which they work almost invariably find that they feel underappreciated and they come away disappointed and sometimes resentful of the

178 /   COURAGE & CALLING

organization. The reason is simple: our workplace will not provide this support.

Often the language of "family" is used to describe people who work together. But organizations are not families; and they cannot be family to us. Families, for example, should never reject one of their own. But in the workplace we are evaluated and reviewed and sometimes we are terminated if our competencies are not appropriate for the job or if finances make termination necessary. People who think of the organization as a family are emotionally crushed if they are terminated; they wonder how they could ever be asked to leave. "After all," they might say, "I thought this was a family."

We will find and should find significant and meaningful friendships in our places of work; in fact our work is more effective when we know that there is at least one other person in the organization who is a friend. But we cannot depend on the workplace to meet all of our needs for community, friendship and emotional support. It is an unrealistic expectation. Consequently, it is essential that we find a breadth of emotional support outside the workplace. This is a key means by which we keep a balance in terms of our institutional loyalties. It is critical that we develop our sense of vocation with *reference* to the workplace but not in *dependence* on the workplace. Jobs are not secure, and our workplace colleagues cannot be our main source of emotional support.

Furthermore, people who are in need of constant affirmation drain energy from the organization rather than bringing strength to it. When we long to be affirmed and supported by the organization, we almost invariably behave in ways that will bring about this approval. The consequence is simple: we are no longer true to ourselves and to our vocation.

A key indicator that we have an unhealthy dependence on an organization is when we are at a loss when the organization does not tell us what to do, or when we feel helpless when the organization does not take us into account in its plans for the future. What has happened is that we have placed the responsibility for our lives in the hands of an organization—essentially giving that organization a parental role—and have failed to take responsibility for our own lives. Many times this is justified with an appeal to faithfulness or perseverance or dependability. But these virtues are noble and mature only when they are accompanied by personal responsibility, courage and conscience.

Ideally we will be 100 percent present while holding to a primary commitment to our own vocational identity, defined in terms of our loyalty to God. We can be fully present, eager and generous participants in the organization in which we serve. But we need to hold our institutional loyalties lightly; the organization is not family, and God's direction in the lives of most people will likely lead them to resign at least once in the course of their career, especially in this new economy. And each time they resign their choice can be one of vocational integrity; it can be rooted in a resolve to be true to their own call.

We can be fully present without unhealthy emotional dependence. But being one hundred percent present *does* mean making a commitment to give our energy to a particular group of people, to a particular organization and mission at a particular time.

Over the years I have spent a great deal of time interviewing and hiring new personnel for the organizations in which I have worked. And I have learned that there are some people who habitually give of themselves only minimally because they are ladder climbing. They are only in a particular position until they can find what they are *really* looking for. This is odious. When I hire I do not expect that people will make a lifelong commitment to the organization. And if I hire good people, chances are that down the road they will move on to other challenges. But while they are here, it is reasonable to expect that they will be one hundred percent present, giving themselves to this mission and to these people at this time.

To resign or not to resign: The tough decision. When, and under what circumstances, is it appropriate to resign from the organization in which we work?

First, it is imperative that we affirm a fundamental bias *against* job change. The virtues of perseverance, patience, faithfulness and dedication are essential if we are going to fulfill our vocation. When we change organizations, as often as not we merely exchange one set of problems for another. Many people's personal strength of character is never adequately developed because they have not worked through situations or problems or crises, but have, for various reasons, always run from difficulty.

There *are* times, however, when we should resign. In the new economy virtually all people who live in faithfulness to their vocation will resign at least once during the course of a career. But the reason for resigning must be rooted in conscience and calling; resignation must be an act of *courage*.

Some people will resign because they recognize that they have completed what they came to the organization to do. Their strengths no longer match the needs of the organization. God called them to a particular church or mission group or business to match their strengths and vision with the particular needs of the organization. And now, before God, they have the courage to see that they have completed what they went there to do. Part of the genius of being effective is to know when to persevere and when to leave, when to work through difficulties and when to recognize that we have reached the limits of our effectiveness.

We should not stay when we are no longer effective. In some cases we will see that what we have to contribute can best be used elsewhere. In other cases, we will see that we can no longer be effective because we do not have the necessary level of support from others, such as our superiors or the board of directors, to be effective in our work.

No situation is inherently hopeless. Rather we should ask, Are my strengths needed in *this* place at *this* time? Will I genuinely be able to see my strengths complemented by those of others to produce a common vision? Many in military circles have noted the wise dictum: "Do not reinforce failure." Surely this principle has significance for our commitment and involvement in organizations. For example, some people begin a business venture only to discover that the venture really will not work, and some people accept a call to missionary service only to discover, hopefully sooner than later, that it is not really their call. Why reinforce "failure"? Rather with humility and courage we can accept that we made a mistake and move on to a new chapter in our lives.

For other people resignation will be a matter of conscience. Perhaps there have been changes in the organization that they cannot, in good conscience, support. Or maybe there are expectations placed upon them that are unreasonable and debilitating. Perhaps they are being asked to perform duties that they cannot, in good conscience, perform. In some cases resignation follows an unethical demand; in others it is prompted by an unreasonable expectation. Either way, the decision to resign is a matter of conscience. My parents, for example, offered their resignation to the mission group in which they worked when they were required to send my sister and me away to a boarding school.

Unfortunately, fear of the consequences can keep us from making a wise choice to resign. There are at least three reasons why people are fearful of resigning. First, we sometimes fear that we will make a mistake. This is understandable. We probably recognize that our motives may not be entirely pure, and we may, with good reason, question our own judgment. And it is wise to have a bias against change and an intentional inclination to stay with a situation, however problematic. Nevertheless, we should not delay unnecessarily. In most cases people who should resign stay much longer than they ought to. They are unfortunately released or terminated long after they should have taken the initiative, or they finally resign when all those around them have known for some time that they should leave. Think about it this way: When it comes time to resign you should be the *first* to know, not the last

A second reason people do not resign when they should is the fear of financial insecurity. We must be wise when it comes to financial management and the care of family and our basic needs. But when this fear keeps us from resigning, it is often because we have unrealistic expectations about what financial security looks like, or because we have placed our lifestyle expectations ahead of vocational integrity. Our sense of financial security or insecurity should have more to do with our heart commitments than with how much money we have.

It is more important to resign a job that provides financial security than to compromise our conscience. The courageous thing to do may be to graciously accept a simple position just to pay the bills rather than continuing in a better-paying position where vocation or conscience or family responsibilities are being violated.

The *International Bulletin of Missionary Research* has an interesting series entitled "My Pilgrimage in Mission." In one of these essays William A. Smalley describes his journey of faith and ministry. At age fifty-four, with a Ph.D. in anthropology and linguistics, he realized he needed to resign his post with the United Bible Societies. He and his wife sold their home and moved into a low-rent apartment, while he paid the bills by working as a clerk in a discount toy store. Later he came to speak of the experience as "a time of learning, growth, and liberation" for him and his wife. He found an academic post a couple of years later that suited his abilities and experience.[3]

The grave danger is that we will make career choices solely in terms of financial prosperity or security, that we will essentially identify our self-worth with our wealth and our capacity to make money. And money is so elusive.

Third, people hesitate to resign when they should because they fear that they will be perceived as lacking the will, the fortitude, the perseverance and the grace to stay with a difficult situation. They fear that they will be branded as quitters and consequently suffer a loss of reputation. But in the end our only hope for vocational integrity is to accept that there will be times when we will make others unhappy and that they may well take out their unhappiness on us. The bottom line is that our conscience is our guide, and it is God to whom we are ultimately accountable.

It is virtually impossible to make a major vocational step our initiative, to embrace what we are being called to do, without at the same time having to let go or lose something else. Resignation will be a "small death." It may mean that we will let go of and lose the respect of certain people. That may be the price of resignation, but it is a small price to pay if we can walk away from a situation with our personal integrity intact.

When we are considering whether to quit or resign from a work situation, there are some fundamental questions we need to ask.

Why would I *not* quit? Because of fears that are not legitimate? Am I hesitating because of nothing more complicated than a desire for financial security? Am I hesitating because of my fear of what people will say about me?

What is motivating the move? Is it anger, frustration or discouragement, a hurt ego because I was passed over for a promotion? Is it an inability to work with others? Am I running from problems or from unresolved conflicts in relationships? Am I inclined to resign because I do not want to accept the limitations of this organization or be accountable to others who will critique my work?

A sure signal that we should *not* resign is when we suspect that it is

WORKING WITH & WITHIN ORGANIZATIONS

really impatience that is driving us. We need to distinguish impatience from the gracious recognition that we can do no more in a situation, that we have accomplished what the Lord brought us to the organization to do.

Finally, when we are inclined to resign, we need to ask: Is my fundamental reason for considering resignation that I know I have to be true to myself? Am I motivated by the recognition that I must live in the truth about my own identity?

When we consider whether we are thinking about resigning in order to run from difficulty, it is entirely appropriate to ask a simple question: Is this a cross, a difficulty that I am being called to bear? God will unquestionably lead us through difficult valleys, but it is always reasonable to ask if this is a valley that he is calling *us* to walk through. Gethsemane was an extraordinary experience for our Lord; he was confronting the Father to verify whether the cross did indeed need to happen. He was not unwilling to go to the cross; rather he needed to know that this was what he had to do—that this was *his* cross.

Sometimes God calls us to stay with a difficult situation; and sometimes he graciously calls us on to something else. This is why it is imperative that we consider the matter of difficulty and suffering as we explore what it means to fulfill vocation within organizations, lest we think that difficulty automatically means that it is time to move on.

Often it is so difficult to know what is right. Indeed, none of the decisions in my life have been anywhere near as difficult as the tough choice of whether or not to resign. Each time, that choice brought me to another level of radical dependence on God and on others. And through each of the transitions I have been impressed by how difficult it is to know when it is time to persevere and when is it time to resign. Rarely is it an easy choice. James Fowler captures this tension well:

> There is likely no area of potential self-knowledge where we are more subject to self-deception and more tempted to resort to self-serving rationalizations than in accounting for our efforts to influence and determine the social collectivities of which we are a part and the lives of those involved in them.[4]

How can we do it? How can we resign with conscience and courage as well as wisdom? How can we be people who are fully and generously engaged in our places of work, but not in unhealthy dependence upon them? How can we sustain a differentiation that will, when the time comes, give us the freedom to step aside and move on to another challenge?

Our only hope is to follow a pattern of solitude that enables us to live with the peace and serenity that comes from God and a pattern of intimate relationships that allows us to discuss what really matters, to discuss questions of vocational congruence and integrity. We need solitude *and* community.

Ten

THE ORDERED LIFE

Between Solitude & Community

*A*nother critical point of leverage in our vocational development is the *structure* of our lives and our days—the way we order our lives. We seek an order that enables us to know and embrace our vocation and to fulfill it effectively.

The Freedom of Order

Order brings freedom. Without order our energies are dissipated and our focus dimmed; we are caught up in hectic, confused activity, or we are left purposeless and confused about our identity and about what to do next. Through order, a gracious routine and rhythm to our days and weeks, we can live with strength and freedom.

Without order deadlines become burdens and time becomes an enemy—something we constantly struggle against and constantly feel threatened by. With order, time is a friend. But order is not synonymous with regimentation or rigidity. The best order for our life is an order that *fits* our life—that is customized to *our* vocation. It is a pattern of life that enables *us* to thrive. The best order suits our temperament, the character of our relationships, the focus of our work and our life circumstances. The order that brings freedom to an artist or a homemaker will be quite different from the order that brings freedom to a dentist or a school teacher. But each person will find freedom through order.

Through order we find the freedom that comes with regular sabbath rest, the joy of a life in which both work and rest are embraced, where the sabbath is indeed a *sabbath* rather than just a day off from work.[1] Through order we come to graciously accept both our responsibilities and our limitations. The order of our lives frees us to respond with grace and compassion to needs along the way without being derailed from our fundamental call. Without order we are left confused and bewildered by competing demands and expectations, by an overwhelming sense of the needs around us, and by our own egos driving us to be heroes. We are left busy people who accomplish little.

Three principles can guide us as we order our days. Some people may consider these principles to be another form of time management, and to some extent they are. But the ordered life results not so much from the management of time as from the management of self. What follows are not time management techniques, but root principles that give us freedom from disordered lives.

The principles of an ordered life presuppose the three levels of understanding with which we think about vocation[2]: the fundamental call or vocation to be a Christian; the specific or unique call on each life, our purpose for being; and the daily duties and responsibilities to which we are called today—our immediate priorities.

Sustain clarity about what is important. First, to live an ordered life we must sustain a clear perspective of what really matters and what is truly important. Invariably, a disordered life is a symptom of a lack of clarity about priorities and purpose.

A "to do" list need not be merely a random identification of things that need to be done. It should reflect priorities—the things that are important and need attention over the long term, things that will never be accomplished if we think and act only in terms of the urgent and the immediate.

Our sense of what is important should be rooted first and foremost in the fundamental call to be Christian. Nothing is more important than our growth in faith, hope and love. At the center of our lives we must sustain a pattern of spiritual discipline and nurture that enables us to be thoroughly Christian.

The important things must also be reflected in what we are called to do now and in the immediate future—whether we are raising children, keeping a house clean or writing a paper. While such activities may not in themselves relate to our fundamental call, they are important. When my sons were children they were, of necessity, a priority. While this does not mean that I did not attend to career or ministry, it was essential for me to remember at that stage of their lives (and mine) that they were a priority for me.

Our daily agenda should consistently reflect what it is that we are being called to do in this place and at this time. In other words, our "to do" list can and should include things that must happen today that reflect both our immediate commitments and our long-term priorities. For example, in my daily work patterns I must keep my attention focused in multiple directions: What meetings are coming up for which I need to prepare reports or agendas? Also, what things must I do today for which the benefits or fruit may not be evident for weeks or even months? As a professor I notice that students complain when assignments for my course are due on the same day as those of another professor. I wonder why that should make any difference. All through our lives we will have to live with agendas that intersect, so we will have to learn to do today both what is immediate and what comes due several days or even weeks from now.

Many people find the dictum "first things first" to be helpful in prioritizing items on a "to do" list. This is a way to cut the propensity toward procrastination that leaves so many people scrambling to meet deadlines.

Graciously accept the limitations of life. Another way in which order brings freedom to our lives is through the gracious acceptance of our limitations. We cannot do all that we wish we could do, and we cannot be all things to all people. So we can stop trying to do everything. We can learn to depend on others by delegating, when that is possible, or by simply accepting that others can and will do things well.

Accepting the limitations of life includes graciously expecting that there will be interruptions, delays and unforeseen developments in our day. As we are often reminded, life is messy. We cannot respond with frustration or irritation every time we get caught in a traffic delay. Life is messy; traffic delays are part of the package, part of owning and driving a car, a normal element of urban living. In an ordered life we must choose to sustain flexibility, a sense of humor and a fundamental patience with ourselves, with others and with life itself.

The freedom to accept our limitations is evidenced in the ability to say no. Many people experience life as one continual burden simply because they are trying to do too much. We accept more than we can possibly do well; we respond to the requests or needs of others, knowing that we are being driven not by "a spirit of power and of love and of self-discipline" (2 Tim 1:7), but by some other propensity.

It is helpful to discern what prevents us from saying no. Some of us fear rejection, and our longing for acceptance drives us to do more than we should attempt to do. Others among us long for a sense of importance. If we are busy, if we are doing many things for many people, we feel worthwhile, important and in control; we feel needed. Still others simply do not know what they are being called to do, and they seem to think that if they do as much as possible they will hit upon what it is that they *should* be doing!

The inability to say no inevitably leads to frustration. We can never do enough to feel that we have done what is necessary to gain acceptance or to feel important. It is hopeless. Our only hope is to come back to a clarity of purpose and call, a sense of who we are and of what we are being called to do in this place at this time. We need to come back to clarity about what is important. And there will be many days when regaining clarity is all that we do. But at least we did what was important.

Therefore, we must resolve before God that we will not take on more work or responsibility than we can fulfill with a calm and serene heart, free of hurry or rushed busyness. This resolve is liberating, and it will keep us from much grief. More to the point, it will free us to live a life that is ordered around who we are and what we are called to be and do.

Create and embrace the spaces in your schedule. Finally, an ordered life includes spaces—times in our days and weeks that are unscheduled and uncommitted. We can intentionally create these spaces, and we can learn to accept the spaces that inevitably come our way—waiting times over which we have little control.

First, create the spaces in your schedule. Create margins in the day between activities; allow time for thinking, planning and conversation in the daily routine. Arrive early to appointments so that you are centered and at peace with yourself as you attend meetings. If you are planning a meeting, plan to end early—before the scheduled adjournment time—so that there is space at the end that frees others from feeling that they need to rush on to their next appointment.

Begin the day with space for prayer and reflection, and as you are planning your day, find spaces in your schedule to collect your thoughts, quiet your heart and respond to unforeseen developments.

Embracing the spaces in the day includes graciously accepting those inevitable waiting times that we do not choose. We can accept them as gifts rather than as burdens or interruptions. When we are stuck in traffic, sitting in the dentist's waiting room or waiting for someone who is late for an appointment, we can graciously accept that waiting is part of life. We can decide whether to allow impatience and irritation to filter into our hearts or to accept a waiting time as a gift—an opportunity to read, to pray or to observe the character and expression of life around us. Or we can just wait, allowing our thoughts to settle on that which is true, honorable, just, pure, pleasing, commendable, excellent and worthy of praise (Phil 4:8).

If followed, these three simple principles—sustaining a clear sense of what is most important and what takes priority, graciously accepting the limitations that come in all of our lives, and creating and accepting spaces in our schedules—will enable us to live in the freedom that comes with an ordered life.

But we must go further. However helpful these three guidelines might be, we still need anchors to our lives if we are to live in an ordered way, able to respond with strength and grace to the call of God and the actual circumstances of our lives.

We need two very particular anchors if we are going to grow in self-knowledge and to have the courage to see who we are and the humility to accept who we are. The same two anchors enable us to come to terms with our fears, to make sense of the difficulty and pain that intersects with our lives and to respond with heart—with emotional resilience—to the changes and trials of life and work. These anchors enable us to live and work with a life-sustaining joy.

Without exception, ordered lives are structured around and anchored in two realities: community and solitude. The one without the other is of minimal value; we need both community *and* solitude.

Community as Conversation

We need the grace of community. We discern our vocation in community, and we fulfill it as we are anchored in mutual interdependence with others within community. Furthermore, we negotiate our vocation with others—with our spouse, with the community of faith, with people with whom we live and work—taking into consideration their actual needs and circumstances. No vocation is fulfilled in a vacuum apart from the needs and experiences of others with whom we live and work. Having a vocation never means that we are freed from the obligations and responsibilities of communal life. *All* vocations are communal in character.

This is not all good news; the community, even the community of faith, can be oppressive. The traditions, expectations and cultural patterns of family and community can easily undermine our capacity to become our true selves and to discern our vocation. Some people may wonder, when they consider their own context, whether it is even possible to genuinely discern vocation in their community; they may well think that their only hope is to get away and find solitude and strength and encouragement elsewhere.

We can so easily get caught up in the expectations of others. We must be wary of people who have something to gain if we fulfill their expectations, who all too easily equate their expectations with the expectations of God, whether they be parents, pastors or other authority figures. There may be times when we need to make a break, if we conclude that personal integrity is impossible because of the oppressive character of a community.

This is where solitude is so critical, for it is in solitude that we encounter the one to whom we owe our *ultimate* allegiance, the one who alone can give us security, identity and purpose. This is why we cannot live merely in community. When we do, we are easily consumed by communal expectations rather than living our life in response to the voice of God.

But even as we recognize the dangers of community and affirm the need for solitude, we must come back again and again to our critical need for

community, for life lived in the company of others. We are not walking—
and cannot expect to be walking—this road alone. Some form of authentic
community is necessary to grant us the capacity to discover ourselves and
to embrace vocation.

By community we mean the capacity to live in *communion* with others.
This communion is a means of grace, and as such it is the very stuff of life.
It is really remarkable that God says that the creation is good, very good
(Gen 1). But he also states that it is "not good" for Adam to be solitary
(Gen 2:18). In other words, Adam needed more than God! He needed the
company of others; only through this company could the radical aloneness
of the human soul be overcome.

It is in community that we learn to honor one another—to honor without
flattery but with a love informed by truth. It is in community that we learn
forgiveness—the capacity to bear with one another, as Christ has borne our
sins and forgiven us. And it is in community that we learn how to serve and
be served, how to give and receive. It is in community that we love and
receive love. Without community we remain fundamentally alone,
one-dimensional and disconnected—not only from others but from ourselves and from God.

Ultimately *conversation* is the greatest gift of community and the fundamental means by which community in the Spirit is attained. It is conversation that sustains marriage, friendship and congregational life; it is
conversation that enables us to work together effectively.

Most of all, though, it is in conversation—with friends and with family
members, with peers and with people who are older or younger than us—
that we grow in wisdom, grace and strength. It is through conversation that
we are *encouraged,* that we fill one another with courage. When we are
encouraged, we are able to overcome our fears or at least keep them at
bay—and know that our fears do not drive the engine of our hearts and
lives.

Conversation involves two simple acts or elements. The first is the discipline and grace of *listening*. There is probably no greater service that we
give one another than to listen. When we listen to others, we attend to them,
honor them, accept them and respond to what matters most to them. Nothing so demonstrates that we love other people as does listening to them.

Of course we listen only when we resist the temptation to say something, to teach something or worse, to tell people what they "should" do before we have really heard them. The death of conversation comes when we speak before we listen, when we speak before others have really spoken, when we jump to conclusions or make premature assumptions about what they are going to say.

Then, of course, conversation includes *speaking*. But speaking must be without innuendo, complaint or sarcasm. It is the word spoken without pretense or posturing, the word that is the truth plainly given, without exaggeration, without flattery.

Some people seem unable to speak without being patronizing; when they speak they are seeking to control or to cover their own fears. It is bad enough to speak to children with a condescending tone; but for some people patronizing speech has become a pattern, a habit of all their speaking. It undermines any possibility for genuine conversation; their words are no longer connected to their eyes, let alone their hearts.

When genuine conversation happens, it is life to us. In the listening and speaking of conversation we have the capacity for intimacy. Through conversation we come to the honesty and humility to accept who we are and to confront our innermost fears, forcing them out into the light and finding that they are not nearly as terrible as we imagined.

Through conversation with another we come to terms with our joys and our sorrows; we acknowledge and live through the pain of anger, mourning and discouragement. Without conversation we are alone—alone in our fears, and worse, alone because we are disconnected from ourselves. Ironically, the truth is that we are connected to ourselves only when we are connected to others; we are capable of true self-knowledge, knowledge that enables us to know and accept the call of God, only when we are in communion with others.

When we are consistent in the quality of our conversation with everyone—spouse, family, colleagues and others—God, in his grace and wisdom, grants us the special friendship of a few people, perhaps two or three. We cannot find intimacy with everyone; we cannot hope to and do not need to share our deepest fears with everybody. But in the grace of God we can respond intentionally to a few people—likely, but not necessarily, our peers—with whom conversation becomes increasingly honest and true, without pretense or posturing. In my relationships with the few men with whom I have this kind of friendship, we can pick up where we left off even when we have not seen each other for a year or two. I count these friendships—just three or four along the way—to be among the most precious gifts that God has given me, second only to the joy I have in married life and as a father.

Solitude

Early in Jesus' ministry, Peter and the other disciples press him to return to Capernaum because of the needs of that city. Without equivocation he advises them that he must go to other villages, "so that I may proclaim the message there also; for that is what I came out to do" (Mk 1:36-38). But lest the disciples conclude that he is heartless and lacking in compassion, when Jesus comes upon a man who is desperately ill and calls out to him, he is filled with compassion. He reaches out and touches the man and heals him (Mk 1:40-44).

What makes this so remarkable is that Jesus had clarity of purpose. He knew who he was and what, fundamentally, he was being called to do. He was not derailed or overwhelmed by the needs of Capernaum. Neither was he caught up in the emotional pleas of his disciples. I once heard the great Scottish-Canadian preacher Glyn Owen put it this way: "It was more important for Jesus to *be* a servant than to be thought of as a servant."

But then we see that Jesus had not only a sense of purpose but something else. We are brought up short by the power of Jesus' encounter with the leprous man. He was *filled* with compassion. The Father did not call Jesus in such a manner that he could not respond with compassion along the way. Neither does any of us have a call that precludes responding with grace to the needs around us, whether attending to an ailing neighbor, paying attention to our children or listening to a colleague who needs an empathetic ear.

Is this not what we want? Do we not long to be people who have clarity of vision and purpose, a clear sense of who we are and what it is that we are being called to do—today as well as over the course of our whole lives? But do we not also long to be people of compassion, who without pretense or posturing engage the lives of others with care? Some people are so single-minded about their call that we wonder if they have any awareness of the people around them and of the real and immediate needs that beckon all of us. Other people are like sponges, uncritically absorbing and responding to the needs around them but with little sense of purpose. In both cases what really drives them is ego—a desire for accomplishment in the former case, and a desire to be needed in the latter.

How can we be both people of purpose, with clarity of vocation, *and* people of compassion? The answer is found at the beginning of the story: "In the morning, while it was still very dark, [Jesus] got up and went out to a deserted place, and there he prayed" (Mk 1:35). It was here that his disciples found him after looking everywhere for him: in solitude.

Solitude is fundamentally a place of prayer—of personal and individual encounter with God. To be in solitude is to be intentionally present to God. Solitude is not the act of being alone; rather it is the event of being alone *with God*. Solitude is therefore the fundamental and most essential expression of Christian spirituality. It is the place, the emotional and spiritual *space,* in which we give our unqualified and undivided attention to the one who calls us. The prayer of solitude is the prayer of conversation. It is the place of honesty before God; it is also the place of the open heart—of responsiveness to the prompting of the Spirit.

Solitude is essential for vocational clarity and integrity because it is in solitude that we are enabled to sustain a connection, a relationship, with the one who has called us. It is through the encounter with God in solitude that we are able to see ourselves in truth and to think honestly and critically about who we are, without pretense or misguided aspirations. In solitude we can come to terms with our emotional ups and downs, be honest about our joys and our sorrows, know grace for the times of difficulty and disappointment, and accept and confess our failures and shortcomings.

Without community, solitude is nothing more than an escape from people and from the pressures and stresses of life and work. Stepping aside may have its time and place, but the danger is that it will become nothing more than self-indulgence. However, when we are people who live in community, solitude is the critical spiritual discipline that enables us to draw on the strengths of the conversation we have in community while avoiding the ways in which community is oppressive.

If *conversation* is the critical means by which we know the grace of community, then the equivalent exercise in solitude is *journal writing*. Journal writing may be nothing more than the written record of our prayers—of what we are saying to God and what we sense God is saying to us. As such, the journal is an indispensable means by which we make sense of what is happening in solitude, develop vocational awareness, monitor our emotional development, process the transitions of our lives and keep track of the critical choices and decisions we make in response to the prompting of the Spirit. A journal, then, is so much more than a mere diary; it is the account of our prayer, of our encounter with God.

I believe it is Tolstoy who once wrote that between the lines of what we write in a journal is the outline of our future. But this is only the case if we write as though in conversation with God. A journal is not something we write with a view toward one day publishing our memoirs. Rather it is a private space in which we can respond with "massive honesty"[3] to God, to others, to our circumstances and to ourselves. The journal enables us to see things as they are. Few things are as effective as a well-kept journal for enabling us to live mindfully, to respond intentionally and to keep our hearts from illusion on the one hand and despair on the other.

Different people will approach a journal differently. But consider the following approach. Take time at least once a week, perhaps even daily, to first identify simply and concisely what is happening in your life. Because you are not writing a diary, this is not the most important part, so it is best kept brief. Then, second, describe how you are *feeling* about these events and developments and what you are *learning*. That is, identify what is happening to you emotionally, including how and when and toward whom you have felt angry, or if you are feeling discouraged or if you are feeling a major loss. But also identify what you are learning, and how it is enabling you to grow and develop either in your work or in your relationships.

What you have written so far is essentially *your* perspective on your life, your side of the conversation, so to speak. This is what you see and feel, and this is what you bring to God. But then it is imperative that you also record what you sense the Lord is saying or impressing upon your heart. The record of this *conversation*—the journal—is a record of your personal encounter with God. To the degree that we write with massive honesty and listen with open hearts to the prompting of God, the journal is one of the most valuable resources we can have for vocational discovery and development.

Courage and Calling

We seek the freedom of order. It is found with careful attention to our priorities, gracious acceptance of our limitations and intentional creation of spaces in our daily agenda. But the anchors that give us stability, in the midst of the turmoil and pressure of daily life, are community and solitude, and the grace that we find through conversation and journal writing. Without these we will be consumed by the needs around us and incapable of establishing priorities or accepting our limitations.

We do not seek order as in end in itself. We seek the order that enables us to live with courage and hope in the midst of a confusing and broken world, to be people with a clear sense of call in the midst of change, pressures and uncertainties.

The two poles—community and solitude—are the means by which we know the grace that enables us to live with faith, hope and love. Community and solitude enable us to be mindful, intentional and purposeful. These are the two anchors that enable us to confront our fears and to live and work with hope. It is through the grace of conversation in community and of the encounter with God in solitude that we can increasingly become people of courage in a disheartening and broken world. These anchors enable us to know and embrace with courage that which we are called to be; they enable us to live and work with integrity, with centered lives that find their focus, purpose and strength in Jesus Christ. For our ultimate goal is not so much to accomplish great things, as it is to be women and men who know, love and serve Jesus. Our final concern is not career or ministry or reputation but whether through the course of our lives we grow in the saving grace of Christ. living and working in such a way that others might know him.

Some of the deepest longings of our heart will *not* be fulfilled in this life; they await the reign of Christ, when justice and peace will embrace. In this life we will always have to set aside much for which we long. Some times our expectations will be dashed. Sometimes even if we have a life rich with opportunity and are blessed with a highly supportive community, the sheer fact of life in a broken world is that we will not be all that we hope to be. I suspect that many, if not most, of these longings, fulfilled and unfulfilled in this life, are a foretaste of how we will live and work in the new heaven and the new earth. I suspect that somehow our vocation is not merely for this life but also, in ways we can hardly imagine, for the life to come.

But in this life we will have unrealized expectations and longings. This does not minimize our life and work now; human life has extraordinary possibilities, even in a broken world. It is appropriate that we should long to make a difference through "fruitful labor" (Phil 1:22). These chapters are offered as encouragement to be all we are called to be. But in the end our freedom comes in joining the apostle as he seeks the ultimate vision—his salvation and the glory of Christ. All that matters in the end is knowing Christ Jesus (Phil 3:7-8).

This vision can and must give perspective to the disappointments, frustrations and setbacks of our lives. And the experience of a life ordered around solitude and community enables us to embrace our vocation in this life and in this world, and to do so in light of what matters most of all: freedom in Christ and the capacity to live and act with courage.

Notes

Chapter 1: The Context of Our Lives & Work
[1]"Toward a Healthy Community: An Interview with Wendell Berry," *Christian Century* 114, no. 28 (1997): 912.
[2]Robert Kegan, *In over Our Heads: The Mental Demands of Modern Life* (Cambridge: Harvard University Press, 1994).
[3]John Calvin *Institutes of the Christian Religion* 3.10.6, trans. Henry Beveridge, 2 vols. (Grand Rapids, Mich.: Eerdmans, 1979), 2:35.
[4]Gary D. Badcock, *The Way of Life* (Grand Rapids, Mich.: Eerdmans, 1998), p. 30.

Chapter 2: Seeking Congruence
[1]Parker Palmer, *The Active Life* (San Francisco: Harper & Row, 1990), pp. 64-68.
[2]David Kiersey and Marilyn Bates, *Please Understand Me: Character and Personality Types* (Del Mar, Calif.: Prometheus Minesis, 1974).
[3]Henri Nouwen, *The Road to Daybreak* (New York: Doubleday, 1988), p. 3.

Chapter 3: Chapters in Our Lives
[1]Maynard Solomon, *Mozart: A Life* (New York: HarperCollins, 1995).
[2]An earlier draft of this paragraph noted that if we make a good break from parents, "the next transition will come more easily and more naturally." But when I was revising this chapter, I realized that, at least for me, the midlife transition was not getting any easier!
[3]Ralph Waldo Emerson, "Self Reliance," in *Selected Essays, Lectures and Poems of Ralph Waldo Emerson*, ed. Robert E. Spiller (New York: Washington Square, 1965), p. 241.
[4]W. Jackson Bate, *Samuel Johnson* (New York: Harcourt Brace Jovanovich, 1975), p. 235.
[5]Tim Stafford, *As Our Years Increase* (Grand Rapids, Mich.: Zondervan, 1989), pp. 62-64.

Chapter 4: As unto the Lord
[1]Thomas Merton, *New Seeds of Contemplation* (London: Burns & Oates, 1961), p. 16.
[2]Simone Weil, *Gateway to God*, ed. David Roper (New York: Crossroad, 1982), p. 83.
[3]To the best of my recollection, Parker Palmer is the source of this saying.

Chapter 5: Thinking Vocationally
[1]David Bosch, *A Spirituality of the Road* (Scottsdale, Penn.: Herald, 1979), pp. 22-24.
[2]James W. Fowler, *Becoming Adult, Becoming Christian* (San Francisco: Harper & Row, 1984), p. 103.
[3]Ibid., p. 104.
[4]A. W. Tozer, *The Pursuit of God* (Harrisburg, Penn.: Christian Publications, 1948), p. 114.
[5]Parker Palmer, *The Active Life* (San Francisco: Harper & Row, 1990), p. 66.
[6]The relationship between our vocation and the organizations in which we serve is so important that it merits an entire chapter (chapter nine).

Chapter 6: Courage & Character
[1]Paul Tillich, *The Courage to Be* (New Haven, Conn.: Yale University Press, 1952), p. 4.
[2]Ibid., p. 14.
[3]W. Jackson Bate, *Samuel Johnson* (New York: Harcourt Brace Jovanovich, 1975), pp. 3-4.
[4]Parker Palmer, *The Courage to Teach: Exploring the Inner Landscape of a Teacher's Life* (San Francisco: Jossey-Bass, 1998), pp. 35-60.
[5]James R. Horne, *Mysticism and Vocation* (Waterloo, Ontario: Wilfrid Laurier University Press, 1996), p. 58.

Chapter 7: The Capacity to Learn
[1]Peter M. Senge, *The Fifth Discipline: The Art and Practice of the Learning Organization* (New York: Doubleday, 1990), p. 142.
[2]Mary Catherine Bateson, *Peripheral Visions: Learning Along the Way* (New York: Harper-Collins, 1994), p. 83.
[3]Sharan B. Merriam and M. Carolyn Clark, *Lifelines: Patterns of Work, Love and Learning in Adulthood* (San Francisco: Jossey-Bass, 1991), p. xi.
[4]Ibid., p. 1.
[5]Ibid.
[6]Ibid., p. 3.
[7]Peter F. Drucker, *Managing the Non-Profit Organization* (New York: HarperCollins, 1990), p. 223.
[8]C. S. Lewis, *Surprised by Joy* (London: Collins, 1956), p. 143.
[9]Bateson, *Peripheral Visions*, pp. 74-75.

Chapter 8: The Cross We Bear
[1]John Ralston Saul, *Reflections of a Siamese Twin: Canada at the End of the Twentieth Century* (Toronto: Viking, 1997), p. 26.
[2]Victor Emil Frankl, *Man's Search for Meaning: An Introduction to Logotherapy*, 3rd ed., trans. Ilse Lasch (New York: Simon & Schuster, 1984).
[3]Stephanie Golden, *Slaying the Mermaid: Women and the Culture of Sacrifice* (New York: Harmony, 1998), pp. 233-34.
[4]Golden, *Slaying* p. 234.
[5]Parker Palmer, "On Minding Our Call—When No One Is Calling," *Weavings* 11, no. 3 (1996): 18-19.
[6]Ibid., p. 22.
[7]In the discussion of emotional health I am fully conscious that some wrestle with long-term depression from which it may take years to recover and then only with professional help. These are those who from the Christian community need not condemnation but encouragement, patience and support as they walk through this emotional valley.
[8]Chapter ten includes a more comprehensive discussion of the place of both solitude and community.

Chapter 9: Working with & Within Organizations
[1]On the subject of working in organizations, there are few resources as helpful as those produced by Peter Senge and his associates. Besides his *The Fifth Discipline*, most notable is the sequel, Peter M. Senge et al., *The Fifth Discipline Fieldbook: Strategies and Tools for Building a Learning Organization* (New York: Doubleday, 1994). These helpful volumes identify

the kinds of practices and perspectives that enable individuals to thrive within organizations. As Senge and his associates emphasize, we need to think *systemically.* We are effective when we see ourselves within a system—a whole and complex network. Senge's work is valuable in large part because it is written for all people who work within organizations. Much literature on the quality of organizations and what makes them effective is written only for those in leadership and management. Clearly these roles have a critical part to play, but for us to thrive in our common efforts all of us need to see what makes for effective organizations. Many of the principles in this chapter are based, in part, on insights from these two works.

[2]G. K. Chesterton, introduction to Charles Dickens, *David Copperfield* (London: J. M. Dent and Sons, 1907), p. xii.

[3]William A. Smalley, "My Pilgrimage in Mission," *International Bulletin of Missionary Research* 80 (April 1991): 70-73.

[4]James W. Fowler, *Becoming Adult, Becoming Christian* (San Francisco: Harper & Row, 1984), p. 109.

Chapter 10: The Ordered Life

[1]Note the distinction between a "day off" and genuine sabbath rest as described in chapter four.

[2]Note the three levels or meanings of the word *vocation* as outlined in the introduction.

[3]See W. Jackson Bate, *Samuel Johnson* (New York: Harcourt Brace Jovanovich, 1975), pp. 3-4

For Further Reading

Bateson, Mary Catherine. *Composing a Life*. New York: Atlantic Monthly Press, 1989.

Bosch, David. *A Spirituality of the Road*. Scottsdale, Penn.: Herald, 1979.

Fowler, James W. *Becoming Adult, Becoming Christian*. San Francisco: Harper & Row, 1984.

Green, Thomas H. *Come Down Zacchaeus: Spirituality and the Laity*. Notre Dame, Ind.: Ave Maria, 1988.

Horne, James R. *Mysticism and Vocation*. Waterloo, Ontario: Wilfrid Laurier University Press, 1996.

Merriam, Sharan B., and M. Carolyn Clark. *Lifelines: Patterns of Work, Love and Learning in Adulthood*. San Francisco: Jossey-Bass, 1991.

Palmer, Parker. *The Active Life*. San Francisco: Harper & Row, 1990.

———. *The Courage to Teach: Exploring the Inner Landscape of a Teacher's Life*. San Francisco: Jossey-Bass, 1998.

———. "On Minding Our Call—When No One Is Calling." *Weavings* 11, no. 3 (1996): 15-22.

Peterson, Eugene H. *Under the Unpredictable Plant: An Exploration in Vocational Holiness*. Grand Rapids, Mich.: Eerdmans, 1992.

Ramey, David. *Empowering Leaders*. Kansas City, Mo.: Sheed & Ward, 1991.

Smith, Gordon T. *Listening to God in Times of Choice*. Downers Grove, Ill.: InterVarsity, 1997.